MEETING MY HEROES
LIFE LESSONS FROM ICONS, CREATIVES, AND EVERYDAY LEGENDS

MATT CARMICHAEL

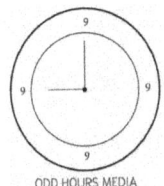

ODD HOURS MEDIA

Meeting my Heroes
Copyright © 2025 Matt Carmichael

All rights reserved. No part of this book may be reproduced in any form without permission from the author or publisher, except as permitted by U.S. copyright law. To request permission, contact Matt Carmichael or Odd Hours Media.

This is a memoir. Each of these stories is written based on the author's recollection of sometimes distant events. While you should read it with appropriate skepticism, he sincerely believes this is how these events transpired. No AI was used in writing these stories, so any hallucinations are human.

Cover design by Clara Davis
Edited by Elizabeth Carmichael-Davis
Published by Odd Hours Media
meetingmyheroes.com

ISBN-13: 978-1-955641-39-5
Library of Congress Control Number: 2025923620

First Edition, Printed in the United States

10 9 8 7 6 5 4 3 2 1

To my family and to my heroes.

CONTENTS

Preface: Cameron Crowe — ix
Introduction: Maria Andersson — xiii

PART ONE
THE VELVET UNDERGROUND

Lou Reed — 3
Moe Tucker and Sterling Morrison — 8
John Cale — 11

PART TWO
OTHER PEOPLE'S HEROES

Jon Hendricks — 17
Keanu Reeves — 20
Dave Brubeck — 22
Mark Grace — 24
Martha Stewart — 27
Rick Steves — 29
Rick Kogan — 32

PART THREE
HEROES OF MY EARLIER SELVES

Robin Williams — 39
Doc — 43
Dr. Welch — 47
Douglas Adams — 50
Marian Rafal — 52
Keith Haring — 54
Ernie Harwell — 57
Mr. T — 61
Boy George — 64
Count Scary — 67
Mojo Nixon and Debbie Gibson — 70
Orson Scott Card — 74

Rickey Henderson	77
Mitch Albom	80
Steve Yahn	83

PART FOUR
WORDS AND MUSIC

John Richards	89
Everclear	94
Alanis Morrisette	96
Joey Ramone	100
Frank Orrall and the rest of the Poi Dogs	102
Nick Tremulis	108
Billy Corgan	110
The Calendar Project	115
The Dead Milkmen	130
Jimmy G. (Not John Cusack)	134
Dicky Barrett and Steven Page	138
Third Eye Blind	141
Wesley Willis	144
Hubert Sumlin and David Johansen	146
Shannon Hoon	150
Tim Harrington	152
Nick Kelly	158
Max Weinberg	162
Kiss	164
Jimmy Buffett	167
Lin Brehmer	172
David Bowie	175
Wilco	179

PART FIVE
PROFESSORS, PEERS AND PROFESSIONALS

Elissa Slotkin	185
Ryder Carroll	190
Lydia Clarke and Charlton Heston	194
My Makers	197
Taylor Welden	205

Ted Allen	208
Richard Florida	211
The New Urbanists	215
The Mayors	219
The Mayors Emanuel	226
Amy Webb	231
The Futurists	234
The Sci-Fi writers	240
Carl Bernstein	244
Nate Silver	248
Edward Tufte	252
The Points Guy	257
Meeting my heroes (my dad's version)	260
Rick Bayless	264
The Storm Chasers	267
Buddy Morris	270
Chuck Klosterman	272
Zoë Keating	274
Amanda Palmer	277
The one whom I didn't meet	280
Epilogue: Career day	286
Acknowledgments	291
About Matt Carmichael	295

PREFACE: CAMERON CROWE

"I wave the flag for journalism," says Cameron Crowe. He's taking questions from the audience at an event promoting the launch of his memoir. The question came from a young journalism student at DePaul. She was wondering what advice he'd have for her. He talked about how journalism is important, though challenged in these times. He also said, "it's a pathway to seek out your heroes."

Cameron Crowe made an art out of meeting heroes. Starting when he was in high school, he found himself in many of the right places and right times. It wasn't just luck, though the fate of coming of age in Southern California in the early 1970s certainly helped. It was a combination of boyish charm, chutzpah, persistence, amazing networking and people skills, and quality reporting and writing that helped position him to write cover stories for Rolling Stone before he was old enough to vote.

The preceding question had also been asked by a DePaul student. She was a film major and asked what advice Crowe would have for a young director. That's because Crowe is an award-winning filmmaker as well and has written and directed stellar films including *Jerry Maguire*, *Singles*, and one of my all-time favorite films, *Almost Famous*.

Crowe waves the flag because journalism was his ticket to... everything.

Almost Famous is a mostly autobiographical film about a young Crowe and his experience on tour with a fictionalized band largely based on the Allman Brothers Band with a helping of Led Zeppelin. You'll read more about what this movie has meant to me in later chapters.

As preface, Crowe's journalism career was a lot like mine. Just at a vastly different scale. Like parallel lines, just really really far apart. He wrote cover stories for *Rolling Stone*. I had photo cut lines in the same publication and bylines for its Web site. He wrote for *Creem* in its Boy Howdy heyday and was mentored by one of the greatest rock writers of all time, Lester Bangs. I wrote for a reboot of *Creem* when it relaunched as a Web site, decades later, helmed by a scrappy new generation. I won't pretend it was the same. I lived in Birmingham, Michigan, so I guess I could have called on Bangs at the *Creem* offices, but he died when I was eight, and *Creem* was gone by the time I started writing for my high school paper.

And importantly, Crowe wrote about rock when rock was everything and yet wasn't at all what it is today. The music was great, as it is now. It just didn't have as much apparatus wrapped around it. The same could be said of journalism. A positive review in *Rolling Stone* or a negative feature could make or break a band. If you were a journalist writing an interview for *Playboy*, a magazine generally known more for its photos than its words, you were required to submit at least 100 potential questions to your editor beforehand. Well-researched, well-documented, probing questions. You would then spend days over the course of months with the subject of your interview. Or in the case of Cameron Crowe, you'd spend 18 months on tour with David Bowie before you wrote your feature. *Playboy*, as a publication, was the real deal and attracted the best writers of its day. I have an unillustrated collection of its interviews on my shelf.

When I came of age as a music journalist, that was... not how it worked. In the mid-1990s, you were lucky if you got 20 minutes on the phone, right after another writer's 20 minutes, and before yet another writer's slot. Now, I imagine it's even worse. Crowe says, during his talk, that Pete Townshend of The Who once spent four hours on the phone with him, knowing that Crowe was only going to file a 400-word column. Must have been nice.

But like Crowe, I wrote about music because I believed in music. I wrote stories about my experiences, and what the music meant to me. I wrote about my heroes and did what I could with the time I was given to tell a good story and humanize all of it.

Crowe said that as a young *Rolling Stone* writer he got called into the office of publisher Jann Wenner who told him he was somewhat disappointed with a highly successful cover story Crowe had just written about Led Zeppelin. He felt Crowe had written the story the band wanted him to write, not the story Crowe wanted to write. He hoped that in the future, Crowe would essentially trust himself to tell his own stories.

I, too, have always tried to get the story, however I could, and tell the best story I could. I won't pretend I ever did that as well as Crowe, or so many other writers before me. But again, I tried. And still try.

Almost Famous debuted at a somewhat pivotal time in my own career. I was balancing freelance rock writing with a day job at *AdAge*, where I wrote about the nascent Internet and how companies used it for marketing. In many ways, the folks leading that charge would become their own kind of rock stars – and I liked telling those stories, too. I took my staff to see the movie as a workday field trip. My friends and I called it "Almost Matt." Because it's the story of how I felt or dreamed my life could have gone, had I made some different choices. Had I lived at a different time. If only...

Do I regret in the end that I didn't try to make that my life, too? Do I regret the "Almost...?" Maybe sometimes. But mostly no. I had some anti-heroes as well. Some archetypes of how that life can ultimately turn out. I mean, Bangs died at 33 while self-medicating for the flu. It's often a lonely life, with long, hard, weird hours. It wasn't a life I wanted to grow old in. At least not in music journalism. Journalism itself... well, yeah, I wave that flag, too. Because the film, and Crowe, were still hugely inspirational in the way I practiced music journalism then, and futures journalism now.

At the event, John Cusack, who starred in Crowe's directing debut, Say Anything, hosted a fireside chat. It was funny, engaging, and charming. He got great stories out of his friend and told a few of his own. I came away with a much more positive view of him than I went in with (see [not] his chapter later.) And I will always appreciate Cusack's Chicagoness and clear love for his city. Cusack said something that struck me. He said it's a revolutionary act to understand all the darkness and choose to be an optimist. It's possible he was quoting something, but regardless, I might have to use that in my next book. That's a very good way to look at what I do today as a futurist.

This book you're holding is a look back. The stories here could be seen partially as thank you letters to all of the people mentioned in it, for all they have given to the world, and especially to me. It's also my way to try and pay it forward by sharing those experiences and the lessons learned.

Crowe said that sometimes you write to "please the little voice inside you that says you have to get the story out." That's part of this book, too. These are stories I have told for decades and some I haven't told before and some I always meant to, and some that just escaped unexpectedly as I started writing. But I eventually listened to the voice and wrote them down.

It was good timing that I got to meet Cameron briefly after the event which took place shortly before my book published, and shake his hand, and thank him for all of the different ways he inspired me. I appreciated the chance to express my gratitude in person. It was the first time I met a hero with the express purpose of including the story here, but it was a perfect encounter to tie everything together.

INTRODUCTION: MARIA ANDERSSON
ON HEROES, AND PRIVILEGE, AND POSTAGE STAMPS

> "Most of my heroes don't appear on no stamps."
> — Public Enemy, "Fight the Power"

This is a book of stories about heroes. And privilege. And for this introduction, postage stamps. I'd been looking for a way to start this collection of stories. As is often the case, music and a shower helped. In this particular case the shower was soundtracked by one of my actual heroes, John Richards, whom we'll meet later.

The set started with Public Enemy's "Fight the Power," followed by the Kinks' "Celluloid Heroes," which includes the lines, "Some that you recognize, some that you've hardly even heard of; people who worked and suffered and struggled for fame; some who succeeded and some who suffered in vain."

I've been thinking about heroes and privilege in writing these stories. Many are stories I've told in largely the same way since I lived them, which in many cases was in my teens and 20s. Looking back, though, I see them from a somewhat, but not entirely, different perspective.

But I'm going to start by giving away the end, because it's so key. The most important thing I've learned is this:

Surround yourself with interesting people.

If for no other reason than they tend to inspire, enlighten and entertain. Interesting people tell, and make for, interesting stories. You'll find life gets pretty boring pretty quickly if you don't work to make it interesting. Find your people.

Scott Smith (@ourmaninchicago) is one of those interesting people for me. A fellow Chicago journalist, we met through Twitter and eventually I suggested we grab lunch at the legendary journalist hangout, the Billy Goat. We've been friends ever since and for a while we were co-hosts of a networking group called Journalist Happy Hour, a torch I picked up from Ted Allen. We had some awesome special guests like John Bracken, John Tolva, Kunur Tucker, Geoffrey Baer and somehow even Edward Tufte. More on that later. This book started as a newsletter idea that I adapted (with permission from Scott).

That's the set-up. Here's the premise.

There's a line people say sometimes that "you shouldn't meet your heroes." They say that because you'll inevitably be disappointed. The theory goes that way because you expect your heroes to be perfect or to always be in character. That's why they're your heroes in the first place, right?

As we put them on their hero pedestal, there's probably even some unfairness to our expectations. Basically there's no way they can be all the things you expect of them when you meet them.

Let's define some terms:

Meeting: I value personal connections and the stories that come from them. That's true of the people who have inspired me, and now even of the products I buy. I think that's somewhat genetic as I think back to being taken as a kid to a Garfield book signing with Jim Davis. If you can meet someone and have that connection, however brief, it brings a different level of appreciation to something. So when I say "meet" in these stories, it's about having a connection of some sort. In some cases they're ongoing relationships. In some cases they're fleeting moments. In some cases they're virtual, like a phone conversation. In the case of Keanu Reeves I didn't actually "meet" him. So I'm drawing the lines broadly to tell the stories I want to tell.

Heroes: I'm drawing this broadly, too. These are people who have inspired me and I've learned from. I believe you can learn from anyone, anytime. And you should. Some of them are people I have long admired for who they are, or what they do, or the way they do it. Some are people I met for a moment, but they got me to think about something differently. Or the encounter makes for a good story. They're all flawed, as people are. Mostly not in ways that take away from the things they have created or done. I hope. I'll admit I haven't researched all of them fully, and not entirely in the context of the present moment.

I don't necessarily want to be like them. I don't necessarily think they are all "role models," whatever that means today.

They're not traditional heroes like presidents or generals or first responders. They're mostly creators of some sort. As this book progresses we'll get into why that is. The answer is basically wrapped up in the other word in the title. They are my heroes.

Getting to meet and talk to interesting people is one of the best perks of being a journalist. I'm also not above just being a fanboy and going to hear people speak or to a book signing. I like having something of a personal connection – even if just for a moment or two. It usually makes for good stories.

I've had good experiences and come away with even more respect for the subjects, with all but one notable exception, whom you'll meet in a moment. It turns out most of the people I most respect are pretty solid humans as well as having all of the talent and creativity I respected. Which leads me to the overarching realization that:

If meeting your heroes is disappointing, maybe you need better heroes.

I say all of that because heroes are important. As the Kinks said, "some of these you'll recognize, some you will have hardly even heard of." Heroes shouldn't only be celebrities or comic characters — though they can be, and that too can make for some good stories.

You also need heroes you can interact with, who inspire you and push you to do the things you want to do better.

Of course, in the end, this is, in an odd way, also my story — and like all authors, I am the hero of my story. So you'll be meeting me, too. But first:

MEETING MARIA ANDERSSON

I think I always understood what a privilege it was to be in positions to meet my heroes. Or to be able to put myself in positions to meet my heroes. I had the unbelievable privilege to not just practice journalism but cover topics I cared about, like music, technology, demographics and, essentially, people.

I like to think I understand privilege with more nuance now. Although I'm still working on that.

For the newsletter version of this project, I created a header image that was a montage of my photos of my heroes. I looked at my little Mt. Rushmore and realized that, like the monument itself, my heroes are predominantly men, and white men at that.

I want to tell more stories of encounters with non-white-dudes. And explore as I go forward why I don't have more of those stories to tell. Some of my heroes have appeared on stamps. Many others look like the people who have traditionally appeared on stamps. Chuck D from Public Enemy can't say that about his heroes. That is, of course, his point.

Which brings me to meeting Maria Andersson. She has appeared on a stamp. She's the singer of a Swedish band called the Sahara Hotnights. I shot them at Metro when they opened for the Mooney Suzuki, posted the photos on rocknroll.net and then kinda forgot about them until I got a really random email from the Swedish postal service.

I've had my photos used in magazines, newspapers, and Web sites. They've appeared in books and on TV and a CD cover or two. Perhaps the most unusual, however, is that they wanted to use my photo of Maria as the basis for an etching done for a Swedish postage stamp.

It was part of a series they issued about the history of rocknroll. The heart of the series was an Elvis stamp. I get how ironic that is, given that I started this piece with "Fight the Power," which contains the line, referring to the King's stamp,, "Elvis was a hero to most, but he never meant [much] to me."

Anyway, besides Elvis, they wanted to celebrate Swedish bands and, I suspect, not just male ones. Sahara Hotnights were getting some attention at the time and they got included. I'll never know how my photo was selected for the basis of the stamp, but it was one of the highest amounts I was ever paid for a single-license of one of my images.

When the band came back around (opening for fellow Swedes, the Hives), I was glad to meet Maria and the others after the show. The stamp wasn't even out yet so they were a little confused by my request: I had them all sign a blank envelope. I later affixed the stamp and framed it alongside the original photo.

INTRODUCTION: MARIA ANDERSSON

Personal connections. People who inspire. Good stories, hopefully well told. Lessons learned. Perspectives examined and even reexamined. That's what this book is all about.

Ready? Let's dive in.

| The full series of Swedish Rock stamps

PART ONE
THE VELVET UNDERGROUND

NONE OF THIS WOULD HAVE HAPPENED WERE IT NOT FOR LOU REED (AND JOHN, MOE AND STERLING)

LOU REED
ON WAITING FOR THE MAN WHO INSPIRED PRETTY MUCH EVERYTHING I'VE DONE SINCE

I was lucky to be at the height of my Velvet Underground fandom and my music journalism career at a moment where the band members were firing on all cylinders – just mostly not together, sadly.

Lou Reed had put out a string of great albums. John Cale was on the road a lot.

Moe Tucker was even touring as a solo act, including a tour with Sterling Morrison.

I met Lou Reed twice. In two very different contexts. He was only kind of a jerk one of those times. But it's important to understand why I met Lou. So let me take you back to my high school band classroom.

I won't say, "my life was saved by rocknroll." But it's impossible to understate the way this black cassette altered my trajectory. Sometimes my brain does a nice job of remembering really important moments, even if they don't seem like it at the time. My friend Anil handed me a black Maxell XLII-S tape (a step up from my usual XLIIs) with Lou Reed's *New York* on it. From there it was all the way down the rabbit hole. I think *Velvet Underground Live in 1969* was next. And then deeper into Lou's solo and the Velvets' catalog. Eventually, as I continued my obsession (as seen in the Daily Northwestern), I got into the bootlegs as well. But being a Lou Reed fan used to be a pretty lonely thing. Even when I went to see him live at Detroit's Fox Theater on the *Magic and Loss* tour I had no way of knowing that Ernesto, who would become a great friend, was only a row away.

That night was the first time I met Lou. Just like any other fan, I waited for the man, outside the backstage door. He came out with an assistant, a Sharpie and a box of 8x10s which he signed for everyone there. He was gracious but not overly chatty. I asked him about a lyric I couldn't make out from the Velvets and he kind of dismissively said he didn't remember himself. There wasn't an Internet really to answer these questions for me.

That would change, and I would help change it.

It all started on Prodigy, the pre-Web dial-up online service. As a huge Lou Reed fan I was mildly irritated that there were like 42 message boards for U2 and none for the artists who inspired them. So I started a Lou Reed board and attracted some people, though not many. Although one was Lisa Robinson?!?

This was 1991.

As the Internet began to take hold, I continued to be disappointed in the lack of Lou/Velvet Underground-related materials. So first I ran an FTP site. Then I started a newsgroup. I want to say I had a gopher server for a moment. And as the first betas of the Mosaic browser started to put a graphic face on the Web, I put together the first Lou Reed Web page with the easy to remember URL: http://daneel.acns.nwu.edu:8081/html/lou/discog.html. I had to compile the Web server myself (with the help of my friends Jon and Jack), since it wasn't like there were any public servers anywhere. It was now March 1994 and the Web was fewer than 3,000 sites old. I posted a note to the Lou list, then run by Anthony J. Rzepela, a man I've never met, but owe much to. And folks from the world over started showing up in my logs. Man, the Internet's cool. We forget that sometimes.

That site certainly changed the trajectory of my life by opening doors, connecting me with new people and fostering an interest in the intersection of music and community, content and technology. Perhaps first and foremost, the late Steve Yahn whom you will meet later.

The site contained, among other things, a lyric archive. Partially crowd-sourced and partially me just sitting down typing up lyrics sheets from the albums. I named my computer after the line I couldn't make out: "gypsy death and you" from "What Goes On." Once Northwestern opened up public servers, I moved it over to a Mac-based web server named Charlotte. And then when I graduated, I found hosts and bought the "rocknroll.net" domain just about two years to the day after the sites launched at NU.

That site became the basis for all that is rocknroll.net now. So how old is this site? Soooo old, that for a while, if you searched the entire Internet for the word "Heroin," this site came up #1 because of the lyric archive. And if you searched for a couple favorite four-letter words, this was in the top five. And I mean, of course, searching with Lycos when it was still at cmu.edu. Or Yahoo! when it was still some Stanford kids.

MEETING LOU REED, TAKE 2

I'd been in touch with Lou's team at his publishing company, Sister Ray Enterprises, about the site. I was trying to get some support for it. At first they made me take down all the lyrics and album covers because of copyright. Which was kind of rude. Although they also put a little effort into trying to figure out how I could get licensed to post that stuff when there were no clear laws about the Internet. I tried to get a photo pass for his show at the Rosemont Theater and they said no, so I just bought a ticket. I again hung out by the backstage door for a while. It swung open at one point and I heard people on the other side searching for a Sharpie. I pulled one out of my pocket and said, "I have one, but I'm out here...." The security guy shrugged and waved me in.

Inside I found my way to the room where Lou and some

other folks and fans were hanging out. Lou was having a cigar and chatting. I approached him to sign my copy of his book of lyrics.

"Hey Lou, I'm Matt Carmichael, the guy who does the Web site about you."

"Oh, yeah I know who you are," said Lou Reed to me.

Let that sink in a moment. As I tried to then.

He signed the book (which I then loaned to Monica who never gave it back and I'm sad) and I asked if I could take a couple pictures.

"For you, or the site," he asked.

"Well ideally for the site, but if not just for me."

"Yeah, sure, but just for you for now... until I figure out what I make of you," he said.

"OK,"

And then he asked me a follow-up question that I still can't get over.

He asked, "Are you a man of honor?"

The thought bubble was all, "Are you serious, Lou? Really? I've devoted countless hours to promoting the gospel of Lou and maybe have almost as big a chip on my shoulder about how under-appreciated you are as you do. Almost."

But I said, "of course," and we shook hands and I took a couple pictures and ducked out.

And that was that.

Around this time I'd started working with Poi Dog Pondering on a site for them. It was...a different experience than this. And so the Poi site took off and I let my Lou site languish – but have kept it running for 30 years.

Am I disappointed that meeting this hero didn't go better? Nope. And it might seem like an odd one to start this collection of stories with, given the idea behind "Meeting my Heroes." But he didn't disappoint. Everyone in music journalism needed a "Lou Reed was a jerk to me" story, and I now had mine. Although, really, he wasn't even that much of a jerk.

It wasn't as if I didn't know better. In addition to reading books about Lou, I had gotten to ask his former bandmates from the Velvet Underground about him in interviews over the years.

Sterling Morrison seemed to want more from the Velvets. He told me, "It sort of pains me. There are a lot of things that we could be doing that we're not doing because of weirdness. Not just Lou's, we're all kind of weird. We always were, and stubborn, and verbal. So some very mean things can get said very glibly."

Moe Tucker was more succinct, "I love him, but he's a pain in the ass."

And when I asked John Cale about working with Lou and if it was tough he said, "Well, I, I... [laughter].... What's done is done."

Through all of this, I learned a lot about the value of harnessing enthusiasm and the waste of not doing so. That was true for me, and I think Lou's bandmates were a little wistful-to bitter there was a lot left on the table for the band itself.

But it's good to understand your heroes for what they are as well as what they aren't. But mostly I learned a lesson I still take to heart: always, always carry a Sharpie.

Here's one of the photos he eventually did grant me permission to use.

MEETING MY HEROES

MOE TUCKER AND STERLING MORRISON

ON GOING WHERE THE STORY IS, AND NEVER BEING SURPRISED BY WHO'S THERE

As I mentioned, in the mid-1990s Moe Tucker was touring as a solo act joined by the Velvet's guitarist, Sterling Morrison.

Lou Reed and John Cale got most of the attention in the Velvet Underground, as the lead singer and songwriters. But Moe's unique drumming and Sterling's guitar, which ranged from delicate to relentless, were essential to making the band sound as unique and timeless as they did.

So I was beyond excited that Moe and Sterling were playing on campus in Madison with Jonathan Richman.

Richman was a devotee and fanboy of the Velvets when he was a young lad and grew up to have his own quirky place in the rocknroll family tree with his band, The Modern Lovers.

Madison was only a couple hours from campus so I begged Linda, a college friend of my dad's who lived near campus, for her car. I promised to return it with a full tank of gas.

My roommate, Jon Michaels, joined me for the road trip.

It was an amazing night in which I got to spend some serious time huddled with half of one of the most legendary bands ever.

Thankfully, I was *on assignment* and wrote it allllll down. This article led with maybe one of the best openings I've ever written.

"'Cornflakes are not the innocent critters they seem,' says Sterling Morrison sagely. He was one of the guitarists for the late Velvet Underground, so he should know these things. We are discussing breakfast cereal. Really. And then the discussion moves on to *Wuthering Heights*. Sterling says that 'Emily (Brontë) was just shooting from the hip.' He has a Ph.D. in English, so he should know these things, too."

They were such a joy to spend time with, and I'm grateful especially to have had the chance to meet Sterling. I was so close to doing so again when he passed away a couple of years later and I was there when Lou dedicated "Sweet Jane" to him at the opening of the Rock & Roll Hall of Fame shortly after his death.

It was interesting to talk to these hugely influential artists in such a small and informal setting.

It comes down to definitions of success, which is always something to think about and sometimes even redefine.

Sterling told me, "The Velvet Underground never set out to be a commercial success. We had built-in reasons why it was impossible. The only thing you can say to our credit is that it didn't stop us. We kept on going anyway." He added that he loved the scale of tours like this, "Playing clubs is great. People come up to you and say, 'Hey, you suck' and I say, 'Well, I did my best.' They tell you what they think and you get to talk to them."

Moe clearly wanted a little more, not necessarily for the trappings of success but because she believed in the music and wanted more people to hear it. She told me, "After a while it became aggravating when you knew there were lots of people who would buy the record if they could find it, but it wasn't well-distributed. That kinda pissed you off when you didn't have money to buy a pair of shoes."

Money for shoes doesn't seem like too much to ask for.

Moe and I met again a couple years later when I shot her show at the long-since defunct club, Thurstons.

Moe has always seemed like such a sweetheart but with a fantastic side of snark. She and I are friends on Facebook, and it was a thrill when she liked the video of baby Meredith singing her signature vocal, "After Hours," which became my eldest's lullaby.

Me, Sterling Morrison, Moe Tucker and... Chad
[Photo by Jon Michaels]

The article I wrote about this trip, and about meeting these two heroes for the campus magazine, *Art+Performance*, remains one of my favorite pieces of writing.

The lesson here is that sometimes you just have to get in the car and go where the story is. Beyond that, just because someone isn't the lead singer, or the main song writer, or the CEO or the star doesn't mean they don't have an incredible story waiting to be told.

JOHN CALE
ON TALENT AND PRACTICE

John Cale was of course one of the original Velvet Underground. His influence is felt in every chord of the first two albums. I interviewed him in college by phone, which was a big deal to me at the time. I was slightly more seasoned when I interviewed him again a couple years later. It was a phoner again, and early on a weekend. I did the interview in my pajamas, before that was a thing that people did all the time when they worked from home.

I remember one story that didn't make it into the piece I wrote at the time. The opening line to his song "Guts" is a caustic commentary on the protagonist's wife. Later in his absolutely flawless live recording, *Fragments of a Rainy Season*, he changed one word that totally altered the meaning. I asked him about it. He said when he wrote the song he was really mad at his recently-ex wife because while he was on tour she sold his piano to buy drugs. Which for anyone is kinda rude. But John Cale is a pianist (and violist and guitarist, but still...) and she sold his PIANO. So yeah, angry lyrics ensued. He'd softened by the time *Fragments* was recorded...

I met him at the Double Door a while later. He signed my copy of *Fragments*, and we chatted a bit. And in one of those Chicago rocknroll moments, I wound up drinking with his band back at the Rock & Rroll Days Inn on Diversey into the wee hours with, as memory serves, Ernesto (whom you met in the Lou Reed story) and Monica (who still has my signed Lou Reed book).

John didn't join us, sadly, because he wasn't feeling well and went to bed to rest his voice. But it was a fun night and the guys in his band were a trip. I wish I could remember their stories better, but that's a function of age and distance, not of the drinking.

Shooting that show, which Monica wrote up, got me my first printed photo credit – in the *Chicago Reader*.

Cale is an artists' artist. He's an innovator to this day, even into his ninth decade. He made several of my favorite records what they are, and *Fragments* would be on my desert island jukebox. Oh, and if you've listened to Jeff Buckley's version of "Hallelujah," it's really a cover of Cale's version, not Leonard Cohen's original.

To me, Cale is an example of two important things. If you're good at something, and I mean really good, you can apply that thing in a lot of different situations. But to get that good, you have to learn the foundations and practice. Cale is a brilliant musician. He's classically trained. But that doesn't mean he just played in orchestras. He took what he learned and basically invented and reinvented and re-reinvented new contexts in which to apply that.

Granted, if you're otherworldly good, you can sometime skip the "learning the foundations" piece — Eddie Van Halen, whom I never met, I'm looking at you – but for the mortals among us and even the geniuses among us, "the basics are the basics for a reason." That last line comes from Buddy Morris, the trainer for the NFL Cardinals, whom I interviewed for *WTF*. Morris was talking about training elite athletes, but it applies in other contexts, too.

Monica, who was a better writer than I, summed it up well: "What saves him from dilettantism is his commitment to whatever mode he happens to be in."

| *John Cale for the Chicago Reader*

PART TWO
OTHER PEOPLE'S HEROES

HELPING PEOPLE LIVE VICARIOUSLY,
AND UNDERSTANDING
WHY THESE WERE HEROES

JON HENDRICKS
ON THE BEST ADVICE A MUSICIAN COULD GIVE

My first-ever celebrity interview was with a jazz singer, Jon Hendricks. My dad introduced me to his music, as with so much jazz. Part of me was excited to get to meet one of my dad's heroes.

I was in college writing for *Art+Performance*, and I was to interview him at the Sheraton in downtown Chicago the night before his performance at Northwestern.

He explained why he was playing Northwestern, and why he had recorded an album called *"Evolution of the Blues Song,"* which was a musical and oral history of the genre. He told me, "You can't educate a child without art. Art softens the sensitivities and widens the perceptions."

I arrived and was told to call his room phone from the lobby, but the line was busy and stayed that way. This was before cell phones. Eventually, nervous that I was now late for my interview, I talked the hotel into having a security guy escort me up to his room. By this time I'm really late and flustered.

Hendricks greets me at the door in brightly colored polka-dot pajamas, with a huge smile on his face and I relax. His wife, Judith, makes me cocoa before she and their daughter, Aria, go to the hotel gym. His family all toured and performed together.

We talked for some time. Or rather I listened and he told story after story about the grand times of jazz and first-hand accounts of working with the masters, and of being a Black musician when there were still restrictions on where they could perform and for whom. And of writing for *Rolling Stone*. And. And. And. My tape ran out after 90 minutes. He kept telling stories.

| Jon Hendricks at the Park West

Judith and Aria were amused, but maybe not surprised, I was still there when they got back.

Eventually, he said it was the best interview he'd ever done because I "just let him talk."

There was a lesson there that I still try to practice. He signed a CD for my dad with his famous "Short jazz poem: Listen." (I might have reclaimed that when my dad passed away.)

That is some fantastic advice right there: Listen.

They say you should never be the smartest person in the room. Because then you don't (or at least you think you can't) learn anything. But whatever room you're in, you do a lot more learning by listening than you do by talking.

I think there's also the flip side to the story. That you should tell your stories to anyone who will... *listen*. If your audience is receptive, keep going.

Also, listen to jazz. His "*Evolution of the Blues Song*" is a good place to start, as is "*Freddie Freeloader.*"

Of jazz he told me, "Jazz is a spiritual, immaterial creation of the sustenance of life. So I think if you respect it, it will protect and keep you and if you disparage it, it will do you in. I have a great respect for music and I expect to live a long, long time and be ageless for a long time." [Note: he passed away in 2017 at age 96.]

I met him a couple of other times, after shows at the University of Chicago, and at Ravinia with Wynton Marsalis (whom I also met that night). It turns out it's easier to talk your way back stage at jazz shows than rock shows. And I met him once again many years later when he was playing with a host of other jazz vocal legends including Kurt Elling. He was always charming. Always seemed to remember me. And I always listened.

KEANU REEVES

ON STRETCHING THE DEFINITION OF BOTH "MEETING" AND "HERO" AND HOW SOMETIMES THAT'S BETTER

When I was in college, I would sometimes — not often enough — come into Chicago to hang out. As I set off to Northwestern, I imagined I'd spend my weekends in jazz bars, hanging out and listening to great live music. That rarely happened. The big reason was a combination of laziness and the Howard L platform. The Evanston Purple Line ended at Howard unless it was rush hour. You'd have to transfer to the Red Line. But the Purple Line didn't run very frequently late at night, so you'd stand out on the Howard platform waiting. And waiting. And waiting.

The Howard L platform is officially the coldest place on Earth. Except in summer, when it is sweltering. It was a very physical barrier. The stop that separated the city from the suburbs.

But one night some friends and I ventured into the area around North Avenue on the border of Lincoln Park and Old Town. There were a lot of theaters along that stretch and somehow we wound up at a bar across from the famed Steppenwolf.

We're there for a little while and in walk two very famous actors: John Malkovich and Keanu Reeves. Malkovich was performing at Steppenwolf, so it wasn't totally shocking, but still, these were some big names in this little bar.

I was actually trying to land an interview with Keanu at the time, which wasn't all that exciting because with the notable exception of *Bill and Ted's Excellent Adventure*, I really really really didn't like Keanu's acting. He wasn't just bad on his own, he was so bad that he ruined otherwise great films like *Bram Stoker's Dracula* because his performances sucked that much. He has since redeemed himself with the *Matrix* and *John Wick* movies and also apparently being an incredibly good human.

I considered approaching him to ask for that interview, not to put him on the spot then and there, but to see if he'd agree so that I could tell that to his not helpful public relations team.

I considered approaching him and telling him he sucked and ruined good movies with his suckitude. He's a famous guy, and rather good looking, so I'm guessing not many people heckled him in bars. Might do him some good.

In the end, however, I just left him alone. Not out of any sort of shyness or fear. *Meeting my Heroes* is full of stories of me wandering up to people and asking them questions or for favors.

No, I left him alone because it was the right thing to do. But at the time, I leaned on that old saying, "If you don't have something nice to say, don't say anything."

More importantly, just leave a poor guy alone with his drink, unless you at least plan to buy it for him.

Well, alone with his drink and John Malkovich.

I never did get that interview. Looking back, not bothering him was likely the right choice at the time. However, Today Me would have worked the "get him to say yes so I could tell the publicist" angle which has worked well for me...as you'll read elsewhere.

DAVE BRUBECK
ON THE IMPORTANCE OF DISCRETION

Another of my dad's heroes was Dave Brubeck. My dad loved his music, perhaps more than any other other jazz musician. That story is simple. The rest of this is going to be a little emotional-roller-coaster. Our relationships to heroes and the contexts we have those relationships in can change, and evolve and contain a lot of complexity. Some humor. Some seriousness. Just like our relationships to each other. That's especially true here because I met Brubeck in an awkward place...

He was at the urinal next to me at Fourth Presbyterian Church in Chicago, where he was set to perform *La Fiesta de La Posada* ("Festival of the Inn"), his Christmas Cantata . Much as I wanted to, I chose not to introduce myself and fanboy. Didn't seem quite the moment to go for a handshake or autograph.

The show was magic. It's an incredible piece of music. In the early days of the Internet, as it was, it was really hard to find a CD copy of it. I eventually did, using a shopping alert on a weird little CD site that I have never figured out how to turn off and still get pings from every few years. But I gave a copy to my dad as a present.

Although I never got to *meet* meet him, I did see him again at Grant Park. And I had a really funny thread on Twitter with DJ John Richards about celebrities you've met in the bathroom. I am not alone in that, either. Oddly this thread tagged Bill Janovitz from Buffalo Tom and Bryan Ferry, whom I also did not take the opportunity to meet in catering at Tweeter Center, but instead Pam and I sat at a nearby table and left him to eat alone. Which I kind of regret, but also could have gotten fired for approaching him, depending on how he reacted. ¯_(ツ)_/¯

In my dad's final moments, we played Brubeck for him. I hope he was able to hear and enjoy.

MARK GRACE
ON MEETING YOUR HERO'S HEROES

If you think meeting Dave Brubeck at a urinal was weird... I met Cubs legend Mark Grace in a shower.

The late, great Jimmy G Galocy, Dag Juhlin, Cubs legend Mark Grace, me, and Eddie Carlson in the shower at the Vic Theater, 1999.

I mean, I guess I probably met him in the hall outside the shower, but still.

We were backstage at the Vic, which is technically under the stage, down stairs leading to a rather cramped basement. Poi Dog Pondering had just performed one of their legendary run of six sold-out nights in 1999. I shot all six, as you can imagine. More on all of that experience later.

Backstage, milling about in the hallway with a handful of my Poi heroes, I found Mark Grace chatting with Dag Juhlin, Poi's guitarist. Of course I knew who Mark Grace was, too. I'd watched him play first base for years. He was there as a Poi fan. And he was signing Dag's guitar because Dag is a big Cubs fan.

I've always been both a Tigers fan (where I grew up) and a Cubs fan. I inherited that fandom from my dad and my grandmother (his mom) who would go down to Wrigley on "Ladies' day" when she could get discounted tickets. When she died, in the height of my baseball fandom, I was bequeathed her subscription to *Vine Line*, the Cubs fan club magazine. And my dad produced broadcasts for Jack Brickhouse on WGN. So meeting a Cub was a pretty big thrill for me, too.

My favorite Mark Grace moment was one I watched on TV but heard in real time. The Chicago Air show was in town and two of the jets buzzed Wrigley Field so close it seemed like they dipped below the light towers. I lived right near the ballpark and heard the roar as they went by.

But the game was in progress and the Cubs pitcher was mid-pitch and therefore sailed the ball just as he was rightly distracted. Mark Grace just ran off the field. It was momentarily chaos and the only time I can remember an ump in a major league game calling a do-over. But I digress.

This meeting in the hall led to our group shower later, because the shower was about the only place backstage that could fit a group — take that as you will. All of this showed me something interesting.

It turns out your heroes have heroes, and sometimes they are mutually heroes for each other because they are both good at different, or even the same, things.

Over the years, I've watched my heroes perform together. Or cover each others' songs. Or in a couple of amazing cases, both. I'll get to those stories later.

I could also talk at length about that run of Vic shows. Somehow it's been 25 years. But the fans that were at the front of the line and later at the front of the stage are still dear friends. Some I met in person for the first time that week. Some I'd know online for years. Some have drifted. Some have left us too soon.

In the chapter about John Richards, I talk about how music can bring people together and the Poi community is one key example in my life. So many connections. Between the fans and even between the band and the fans. Poi is a really special group of people. You'll get to know them more as this book progresses.

But I'll keep coming back to this point. That music and stories bring us together as fans with a common interest and common stories. Meeting those that share in the community is, at the end of the day, even more important than meeting the heroes who sing the songs, or play the guitars, or play the game well.

Meeting both, however, is the best of all.

MARTHA STEWART
ON WHEN YOUR PUBLIC AND PRIVATE PERSONAS CONFLICT

Martha Stewart at her book signing at Borders in Chicago.

Once upon a time, when I was a young music journalist and working at *AdAge*, I spent a lot of time in New York City, where we had a big office in the *Daily Planet* building. The cool thing was that if there was ever a reason outside of work that I wanted to go to NYC, I could just schedule a bunch of meetings and head there.

So one day I got invited to a Yahoo! event featuring performances by David Bowie, Alanis Morissette and a couple of other musicians I really liked. It was in New York so I sent some meeting invites and booked my trip.

One of those meetings was, of course, with my editor at the time. He'd just interviewed Martha Stewart at her office that afternoon. He said she was icy and could shift between that and her public persona as an elegant, well-mannered hostess in a flash.

And then a funny thing happened. I'm in the VIP area before the show later that night and lo and behold, there's Martha Stewart!

My mom loves Martha Stewart. Cookbooks, design shows, *Martha Stewart Living*, you name it. If Martha's involved, she will think it's a good thing. ("It's a good thing" is a Martha catch phrase.)

Martha was chatting with a small group of people and generally in these situations, you're supposed to leave the VIPs alone and ignore them. Because of course you're all in the VIP area together so you're supposed to pretend you're just as cool as they are.

But unlike with Brubeck, I saw my chance, and tapped her on the shoulder. She turned on me and in her eyes I could tell she didn't appreciate me doing so but also was conflicted because she is the consummate hostess. She had to be polite even as I was breaking some social norms.

I had asked her politely to sign my program for my mom and she did and went back to what she was doing.

My point here, and this will be a bit of a recurring theme, is that good (or those who pretend to be good?) people like to be helpful. Sometimes, maybe even often, you have to ask for that. Sometimes that means you have to be bold. But it also means that when people tap you on the shoulder, and when people ask for your autograph, you have to put on your best Martha Stewart and pay it all back.

Later I got to meet her again when I was assigned to shoot her book signing. I did not bring up our first encounter.

RICK STEVES
ON HOW SOMEONE ELSE'S HERO CAN BECOME YOURS, TOO

Sometimes it's unclear why someone is a hero. Why, for instance, would a shark from IKEA suddenly develop a fascination for a guy who writes European travel books? I mean, yes, Rick wrote a guide to Sweden and mentioned IKEA in it. That, it seems, was enough. And thus began Neptune the Blahaj's obsession with Rick Steves.

Neptune joined our family in January 2023 after a period of intense lobbying from Jane. And that fall, after discovering the IKEA/Sweden reference, Neptune started sleeping with Rick Steves' books. He read to me at bedtime. And demanded that I feed Rick. Threats were made. And it's a good idea to take threats seriously when they come from an obsessed apex predator.

I knew Rick Steves from the first time I visited Europe, traveling with my sister and brother-in-law who lived in Italy at the time. We used his books to help us navigate and it all went well, except for that one hotel....

So when Rick was announced as a speaker at the Travel & Leisure show, we picked up some tickets as a birthday present to the shark. Neptune and I emailed Rick in advance to let him know to expect an unusual fan.

The whole family went to the convention center to hear Rick, as we had done the previous year for someone you'll meet in a later chapter. We got there early, staked out the book signing area and got our seats. Rick came out beforehand, but we failed to jump fast enough to go introduce him to his fan.

Rick showed us highlights from his European travel and outlined his philosophy of exploration. He also talked a lot about the tripod of his business model. He speaks. He writes books and produces TV shows. And he runs his own travel business, which he informed us is where all the money is. He also seems to be a genuinely good human. I also respect his "no checked bags" approach and that he has his own line of bags that meet his specifications.

Normally at this event speakers go to a book signing table after their talks, so we pre-bought one of his books so we could hop in the front of the line.

Rick, however, handles things differently. During his talk he said that he'd stand in the back of the speaker area and turn in a circle signing anything people handed him until he ran out of people or got dizzy. He doesn't personalize or take questions and definitely no posed photos. Undaunted, Neptune took our fresh copy of Rick's Rome travel guide. Rick did just as he said, and Neptune orbited Rick, getting the book signed and posing for a photo as Rick twirled in the background. Later, we got another selfie with cardboard Rick, who was easier to pose with. And we got a delayed but very kind note back from Rick's staff after the event.

I've now written two books (this one included). I've done a fair amount of public speaking professionally: about the first book, about demographics, about cities and urban planning, about consumer trends, and about the future of things. I've given talks to audiences large and small, coast to coast and now internationally as well. I've done plenty of media interviews. I've been on MarketPlace and On Point with Tom Ashbrook and the Brian Leher Show. All of that might seem odd for an introvert, but there's a weird irony that some introverts are often more comfortable in front of 500 people than five.

I've always done that as part of my job, starting back in my first tour at *AdAge*, when I was on TV talking about Super Bowl ads.

Thus I have a ton of respect for people who manage to speak and write full time. You'll meet some more of those folks later.

So I share in Neptune's admiration for Rick Steves and was glad that our shark friend inspired us to go meet him.

| Rick Steves meets his biggest fan

RICK KOGAN
ON HISTORIANS AND HISTORY AND SEIZING THE PRESENT

Once, I got to introduce one of my parents to one of their heroes. Because sometimes meeting your heroes is as easy as buying a ticket.

My mom talks about Rick Kogan the way I talk about John Richards. That's the thing with radio: it's so personal. Just their voice in your kitchen or living room or ear buds. It's easy for their voice and stories and baseball calls and music to live in your head. Garrison Keillor was like that too, until he wasn't.

Rick Kogan is a Chicago institution. Both at the *Chicago Tribune* and on WGN radio. He's a second generation newspaperman. His dad co-wrote Lords of the Levee, which is an amazing history of Chicago's 1st ward politics, centered on the colorful Bathhouse John and Hinky Dink. His mom also worked for the *Tribune*. He counted as friends and collaborators the likes of Royko, Ebert, Siskel and Studs. Kogan tells stories of the present, too of course. And he especially likes telling the stories of other story tellers, like the piece he wrote about the Frunchroom, a South Side story-telling series my friend Scott hosts.

In short, Rick Kogan is a storyteller's storyteller. He's the last of greats still standing and has had what must be the bittersweet honor of crafting the obits for many of those legends around him.

He is better off for having this colorful city to chronicle, and Chicago is better because he tells its tales.

One weekend he was hosting a bus tour of Chicago journalism history and I got tickets for my mom and myself for Mother's Day/her birthday. She came out for the weekend. If you have met my mom, you'd know how much she loves history, especially local history. She loves connecting family stories to the events that were happening around them.

The tour was supposed to start in the suburbs somewhere, really early in the morning. People would ride a tour bus downtown, meet up with Kogan after his "Sunday Papers" radio show in WGN's studio at Tribune Tower and then carry on from there. I asked nicely if we could skip the bus leg since it would mean getting up stupid early just to drive out of town and take the bus back. Instead we would meet the tour at WGN.

That turned out to be a great bonus, not only for extra sleep, but because we were the only ones at the studio, so we were invited into the booth while Rick finished up his show.

Which was pretty darn cool, if you ask me. Or my mom.

We met and chatted with Rick until the bus with the rest of the tour group arrived and then we all drove around Chicago together. A lot of the tour was history that has been lost to history. Sometimes the buildings... "Here's where the *Chicago Sun-Times* was..." Sometimes the publications themselves, "Here's where the *Chicago Daily News* was..." and oftentimes the people, "Here's where we illegally spread some of Studs' ashes..."

We saw the watering holes. The hangouts. Both the places where people who made news gathered and the places where the legends who chronicled that news congregated. Which is probably the right word when it comes to journalists and places like the Old Town Ale House. Or the Billy Goat Tavern, where we had lunch with the Goat himself, Sam Sianis. These are places that are not just bars, but take on a holy significance in the lore of Chicago journalism.

Our tour wound up at the Tribune Tower, where we got a Kogan's-eye view of the lobby with its bust of Colonel McCormick. And the office that once was home to Ann Landers. We saw Kogan's desk. And Greg Kot's. We got to go on the upper-level porch beneath the flying buttresses of the gothic gem that is Trib Tower.

Not on the tour were the offices of Tribune Media Services, which used to oversee all of Tribune's syndicated offerings like comic strips, columns, and newswires, among other assets. One of those assets was a very old computer which ran the news ticker in Times Square. And, in that office, I worked one summer moderating content on Apple's fledgling, still-in-beta, never-really-madit-online service, eWorld. I worked evenings after my summer day job at the Northwestern computer labs. Two or three times a week I'd come downtown and get to work in the tower. I'd walk past the exterior, which is studded with bits of other historical buildings, procured by Tribune correspondents the world over. I'd walk through the lobby covered in quotes about the importance of truth and reporting. In short, I spent a few months working in the same building where so many of these folks worked. I even "covered" one of the biggest odd news moments of the era, chronicling the OJ Simpson Bronco chase on eWorld in what was possibly the most trafficked bulletin board that service ever saw.

As a young Medill kid, working there was magic. And also surreal, as it was just as things were about to pivot. A time when an intern could wind up hosting his boss and her boss and his boss and his boss to show them what the Internet was and how it worked. Because yeah, that happened.

I took my family to that lobby while it was still the Tribune Tower. Because that building too is now in the column of Chicago journalism history, not present. Sold off, and converted to condos.

I wanted them to see it. To read the quotes. To have a little of that magic in them.

And to feel it.

If Kogan teaches you anything, it's to respect the historians as much as the history. That the story tellers have their own stories. And to seize those stories while you can.

Rick Kogan (and my mom) at what every reporter's desk should look like, in the Tribune Tower

PART THREE
HEROES OF MY EARLIER SELVES

I HAVE DONE A LOT TO IMPRESS MY YOUNGER SELVES, BUT THEY HAVE IMPRESSED ME, TOO

ROBIN WILLIAMS
ON SEIZING THE DAY

I grew up watching *Mork and Mindy*, which oddly was a spin-off of *Happy Days*. I assume the episode where an alien visits the Cunninghams was after the show "jumped the shark." But Mork was an alien played by Robin Williams, one of the most amazing comics and actors ever.

My younger self memorized Robin Williams' routine, "Live at the Met." Night after night I listened to the cassette on headphones after bedtime. Tethered to the boombox radio by my bed. A lot of it was over my head at that age. Years and years later I was still finally understanding some of the jokes in moments of inappropriate enlightenment. But man, it was always funny.

Later, I watched his movies and was amazed at his range and talent as an actor. From a serial killer to Mrs. Doubtfire, the guy could do it all. *Awakenings. Dead Poets. Good Will Hunting.* Amazing films, all. He was a solid human, too, co-founding a charitable organization called Comic Relief.

I always said that if he did stand-up again I'd get on a plane. In the end, I didn't have to. He opened his 2002 tour in Chicago and I procured tickets and third-wheeled Sean and Erin's anniversary date. Sorry, not sorry.

| *Robin Williams*

Later a crazy thing happened. I was hired by Getty to shoot Robin Williams receiving a career achievement award from the

Chicago International Film Festival in 2004. As a huge fan, I was thrilled and couldn't believe I would get paid rather than have to pay for this gig. I shot the red carpet arrivals. Then his acceptance speech turned into 15 minutes of stand-up, because of course it did.

After his speech, he came into the crowd to cut a birthday cake they had brought in for him in the center of the auditorium. At the same time, I was cutting across to the other side of the venue for a different angle. There was no way to avoid it. Our paths were going to cross.

I'd heard that during his legendary *"Inside the Actors Studio"* appearance, host James Lipton had said that he had always dreamed of going to Williams' alma mater and my rival school, Detroit Country Day. Supposedly, Williams responded that he had always wanted to go to Cranbrook (my high school). I have not been able to corroborate this but I will believe it's true because it's amazing.

As we briskly walked by each other, I said to him "I'm sorry you didn't get to go to Cranbrook." He looked at me like, "where on earth did that come from; I wish I had time to let you explain," and then he was off again. But for one tiny instant I managed to knock one of the most frenetic people ever literally off his stride. I couldn't be more proud.

In *Dead Poets Society*, Williams plays a teacher at a school not entirely unlike Cranbrook. During his first class, he quotes Robert Herrick to his students, "Gather ye rosebuds while ye may." And ties it back to Horace's "Carpe Diem." The latter I translated myself in Doc's class: Seize the day. This concept shows up in stoicism, also from our Roman friends. Memento Mori: Remember that we must die. I have a coin that says that. But its flip side flips that. Memento Viveri: Remember, too, that we must live. I find it's good to remember both.

Because sometimes you don't even get a day to seize. Sometimes it's just the briefest moment in passing. With Robin Williams, seize it I did. And I'm glad. Because I would like

MEETING MY HEROES

nothing more than to have the chance to explain that comment to him, and now I never will.

A great teacher will teach you a lot more than just their assigned subject. Not all of the learning will happen in the classroom. Some of my favorites were: Mrs. Gibbs and Ms. Mosner; Mrs. Appleman, who shared her personal creativity with me to inspire my own in 2nd grade; Mrs. Sneed. Mrs. Lamb and Mr. Lamb. Mr. Hazard. Mr. Twedt. Mr. Mogul, Mr. Schultz, Ms. Matson. Mr. Smart, who wasn't just my art teacher and first boss (at Day Camp) but was my mom's teacher, too; Mr. Cooper, who encouraged my photography; David Watson, the muckraker advisor to my high school newspaper, when I was co-editor; Mr. McColl, my most *Dead Poets* teacher who treated us like grown-ups and taught us history through art and literature; some teachers who believed in me and some whose disappointment in me encouraged me to strive harder just to "show them."

But the next two folks you'll meet did or said something... even something tiny, that changed who I am and how I got here.

DOC
ON PASSION AND ITS APPLICATIONS, AND NURTURING STRAYS

| *Doc, bewildered that I was actually graduating*

I had a lot of amazing teachers. But as a student, if you get even one who is anywhere near as special as my high school Latin teacher, Stephen "Doc" Rosenquist, Ph.D., you will be lucky indeed.

I suppose I met him on the first day of school my freshman year. Latin 2A was a small but staggeringly intelligent group of humans who went on to lead fascinating lives. Doc lived in the freshman dorm on campus and I remember visiting his apartment early on. His cat Athena (she was grey, like the goddess' eyes) took a liking to me. Which flabbergasted Doc. Athena was a rescue and was exceedingly skittish around other people. Her vote of confidence, I think, was important in winning over Doc, much more so than my grades in Latin ever could.

I wrote the following on Facebook when he passed away, and it was later read at his memorial service on campus:

For four years, I spent an hour of the day in Cranbrook's Room 111 earning a steady diet of Cs. It was an anchor, weighing down my GPA and my hope of getting into the College of my Choice. I could have quit at any time -- dropped out of Latin and taken a class that I was interested in. Because, to be honest, I wasn't entirely into studying a foreign language and a dead one at that. Yet every fall I signed on again. You could say that my teacher was a failure. That if, after all that time, I still didn't have a great grasp of the subjunctive mood, he wasn't getting through to me.

But that guess would earn you even lower marks than I did on my weekly vocab quizzes, or on the AP exam which he really couldn't have prepped us better for.

Doc, my teacher all those years ago, was unlike any other. He was a man of extremes. He smoked to extremes: Gauloises, the Jolt Cola of cigarettes, with all the tar and twice the nicotine. He drank coffee to extremes. He collected stray cats and stray students to extremes and nurtured both with equal zeal, making sure that we would eventually be fit company and not so shy and mistrusting of others. He taught five classes with five preps, a rather unheard of course-load.

I think when most people think of "Latin class" they think of dusty books and dusty teachers, dryly declining. 'Discipline' is a word derived from Latin, after all, and with its connections to

Catholic schools as the language of dogma, one assumes that discipline and Latin remain intertwined.

Not in room 111. Or in room 112, for that matter, where the outbursts from next door would cause Monsieur Dagbovie, the neighboring French teacher, to glance over his shoulder from the blackboard, staring at the back wall and shaking his head. At times he would actually come knock on our door or lean out the window to see what the ruckus was.

When he looked in at the daily play going on, hour after hour, through Latin I, II, III, AP IV and AP V, he might have seen Doc banging chalk on the blackboard, or kids playing cards under his desk, or Doc passionately explaining how the use of the ablative case changed the meaning of a line in Horace's *Odes*, or the kids sitting up in the window sill seemingly not paying attention. Someone walking down the hall might, on rare but special occasions, find Doc standing with one foot on each door knob, swinging back and forth and making monkey noises – all so he could fit in better with the circus/zoo inside his classroom.

Commotion, there's another good Latin-derived word.

All the while, he was teaching. In that classroom and especially beyond it. Teaching Latin, for sure. Teaching about having passion, even for a language long given up for dead. Teaching about the extremes you'll go to for that passion. In my case, he once told me that he was envious of the fact that I could prioritize in my own life. If something was important to me, I could drop everything until it was addressed. He was telling me, essentially, that he understood why I wasn't getting As. He might prefer if I "applied myself" more, but he knew I wouldn't, and that maybe that was OK in the long run. He couldn't do that. Doc was binary. Every dial was set to 11 or zero, every day. Every day was coffee, class, coffee, class, smoke, cats, class, smoke, bridge, prep for tomorrow, smoke, cats and maybe eventually sleep. I think he had to give much of that up at some point. Not cut back. Zero. And somehow he also fit in making a profound difference in people's lives.

The testimonials that started rolling in after his passing this week show the impact he had on his students, not just for the minutes in his class room, but throughout their lives. Refrains of "he saved my life" echo in the comments on Facebook. "He listened." "He fought for me." "He taught me how to be myself." I can't think of many teachers who were as beloved by the students getting Cs and Ds as those getting As. And to that end, I'll share one more story of my own.

It was always a bit of a mystery how I got into Northwestern. Let's just say I was a borderline candidate to be sure. My GPA could have been higher, and likely would have been if I'd dropped Latin. Doc knew I wanted to go to NU and without prompting of any sort, just out of the blue wrote them a letter about why they should accept me. Not part of my formal application. Just an outside voice. A letter of support from the teacher of my weakest subject. He signed it "Stephen Rosenquist, PhD" because those letters mattered and were a sign that he knew that education, that learning and teaching, mattered. Though I'll never know for sure, I suspect it made a difference to Shep and the folks at admissions. Regardless, it made a difference to me.

RIP, Doc. Ad astra per aspera.

[Side note 1, take pictures with the people who matter in your life. You won't regret it.]

[Side note 2, my eldest somehow wound up taking four years of high school Latin. I can hear Doc's staccato "HA!" at the thought of that. But I'm not sure what he'd make of the college essay they wrote about how their favorite piece of media is the Wikipedia page for the phrase "ad astra." Life is a funny place.]

DR. WELCH
ON TURNING DISAPPOINTMENT INTO FUEL

This is a story of a great piece of advice, and one of those nudges that can change your life.

Dr. Jeffrey Welch was my freshman year English teacher and my advisor. He was wicked smart, super literate and didn't put up with my slacking. Yes, I slacked. He once commented on an assignment I turned in: "Were you watching TV when you wrote this? Were you alive?" And he wrote something about continuing to water my word hoard so it would grow, etc.

The reason he was hard on me (I think? I hope?) was because he knew I could do better, but wasn't trying very hard.

One of the most frustrating things for teachers (and parents) is dealing with the kids who aren't living up to their potential. This is a clichéd thing to say, but it's true. It's truer now than ever. The world needs smart kids who will grow up to be smart adults. Every bit of that potential that's wasted means one fewer person who can help solve some of the monumental problems coming generations (and the rest of us) will face. Big problems need big brains, working together, to solve them. Those problems will require math, and science, and good writing and communication to solve.

Dr. Welch, impressed that I turned out OK in the end

Somewhat related, I often think of an important, prescient and evergreen piece of advice he once gave me:

"Protect yourself from the idiots."

That feels as if it's getting harder and harder these days. The idiots are everywhere, it seems, and they have figured out how to cheat their way to victory.

Even as a futurist, it's sometimes hard to imagine the future we're facing, but I have to believe that in the end, the smart folks will win.

Dr. Welch is also included here because of a simple thing he said to me in passing once that completely changed my life.

It was my junior year and I ran into him in the math hall. We talked about the student newspaper, which I'd started writing some stories for. I mentioned that I was going to apply to be an associate editor. He said, "Why not editor-in-chief?"

That's the thing about great teachers. They push you and challenge you. He wanted me to live up to my potential and knew that with the right nudge I could maybe pull it off.

When a teacher tells you you're good at something — believe them. Even, or especially, if you're unsure yourself.

Likewise, sometimes a teacher (not a good teacher, mind you) will tell you that you're not good at something, or not cut out for something. If you disagree, double down, push yourself and there is nothing more satisfying than showing them up when you succeed. More on that soon.

Dr. Welch got me thinking. The newspaper has a small staff, probably not too many applicants and often multiple people were "chiefs." My odds weren't bad. It would be an interesting experience, and frankly look good on my college applications.

So I applied, and got it — I was one of three "chiefs" in the end. Thus began my journalism experience, which I loved, and led me to apply to Medill at Northwestern. Which led to all sorts of other things.

In today's world, there was a lot wrong with that picture.

I didn't really have much experience but I went for the big job. There's a lot of privilege involved in all of that scenario, not the least of which being that it took place at an exclusive private school. That privilege was a gateway to others, which were in turn a gateway to still more.

But privilege is only part of the battle. It can certainly open doors. But you also have to be prepared to take advantage of the opportunities presented to you. Sometimes you still have to make your own. Then you have to work hard to earn the place you've landed in.

I'd like to think I put in my hours at the paper and that we put out a decent product that helped inform and entertain our community. I realize I'm making too big of a deal about it, too. But in the moment, it meant something, and long term the experience meant something to me, too.

DOUGLAS ADAMS
ON KNOWING WHERE YOUR TOWEL IS

When I was a freshman in college I went to a book signing near campus at one of Evanston's many now-closed bookstores: Kroch's and Brentano's. The author Douglas Adams was reading from his latest, *Mostly Harmless*. It was part of the amazing "trilogy" of books called *The Hitchhiker's Guide to the Galaxy* which I read and read and read again during middle and high school. I cannot recommend it enough. It has some of my favorite lessons about life, poetry, friendship, mattresses, dolphins, ballpoint pens, space travel and fear.

One of the things that struck me early on was a theory about hitchhiking across the galaxy. As I've said, you should always have a Sharpie. But Adams, through his character Ford, took that a step further. He had a satchel (which I thought was cool) and it was full of things he'd need on his travels. One of the things was a towel.

From *The Guide*: "a towel has immense psychological value. For some reason, if a strag (*strag*: non-hitchhiker) discovers that a hitchhiker has his towel with him, he will automatically assume that he is also in possession of a toothbrush, face flannel, soap, tin of biscuits, flask, compass, map, ball of string, gnat spray, wet weather gear, space suit etc., etc. Furthermore, the strag will then happily lend the hitchhiker any of these or a dozen other items that the hitch hiker might accidentally have 'lost.' What the strag will think is that any man who can hitch the length and breadth of the galaxy, rough it, slum it, struggle against terrible odds, win through, and still knows where his towel is is clearly a man to be reckoned with."

This all informs my thoughts on Everyday Carry (EDC), but we'll get to that later.

But anyway, there was a strict "buy a book get/one thing signed" policy. I cheated and had brought a small index card so after he signed my book, I asked if he'd sign that too.

I've gotten to experience a lot of things that others haven't and meet people others don't get to meet. I can't always bring people with me. But the reason all of these people I meet are important to me is usually because someone I know said, "here, you should listen to this." Or "you should read something by so-and-so." So I try to give back – a photo, or something signed, whatever – to let those people know I was thinking about them, and appreciate that they introduced me to something that touched me.

It's like sending them a postcard.

This card was for a friend who lived in a city Adams wasn't doing a signing in. He graciously signed it, because heroes are gracious to their fans. He then signed a towel for the people behind me. I was jealous that I hadn't thought of that myself. I realized something important: Creative people inspire creativity in others.

Listen to your muses. Be inspired by them. Whatever kind of thing you choose to create as you grow up, embrace it. And then try to inspire that in others, too.

MARIAN RAFAL
ON LIBRARIES

To the surprise of no one, I was quite a reader when I was a kid. I'd be shocked if there were many writers who wouldn't say that.

The day after Christmas was a family holiday, too. Not Boxing Day like the Canadians had, but Bookstore Day. We'd go shopping, first at Eye Browse, the bookstore at the strip mall across the street, and later at Borders in downtown Birmingham. We'd take advantage of half-off prices on remaining calendars, and spend whatever cash we were gifted on whatever books Santa didn't bring us.

But most of my reading happened thanks to libraries. That started with Mrs. Stone, the librarian at Brookside, my elementary school. It carried over to high school with Mrs. Reelitz.

However, the librarian who made the biggest difference for me was Marian Rafal at the Bloomfield Township Public Library. I was vaguely aware at the time that "Marian the Librarian" was a reference to *something* even if I didn't know The Music Man itself.

As kids, my sister and I would ask our parents to go to the library and try to make sure we went when she was working. We would follow her around the Youth Room and she would just pull books off the shelves and put them on the stacks we were carrying until our arms were literally full.

She seemed to love that we were readers and wanted to make sure we were reading a good mix of classics and new authors. As my kids became readers, it was fun to pass along some of her recommendations. Like John Bellairs, or Paul Zindel or Gary Paulsen.

During the pandemic, I attended a virtual book signing with Gary Paulsen, one of the most prolific authors ever. Even his publisher wasn't quite sure how many books he had written but it was more than 200! Talk about "avoid not writing"!

During the Q&A he talked a lot about his experience with libraries as a kid. They were his literal sanctuary. They are my happy place to, especially for focused writing like books...

Marian was fun and funny and encouraged us and enabled us. As much as I'm invested in writing this chapter, I think my sister would write an even longer one.

She encouraged my whole family and that, I suppose, encouraged further generations. My sister and I would both wind up working as pages in that library, shelving books and generally keeping things in order. My dad would be elected to the Library Board. Liz would much later be appointed to her Library Board.

Andrew would get a "job" at the Oak Park Library when he was very young, crawling along the floor of the library, using a yard stick to poke under the bookshelves and find lost books. He found...a surprising amount of otherwise "lost" volumes. He got a name tag and everything, and was paid in beads.

Now my eldest is president of the Teen Advisory Board there, too.

Being a reader is a super power – and also just the best entertainment and most effective and efficient way to learn, as Tufte has taught us. Marian's joy was contagious and its legacy keeps my family in books all these decades later.

KEITH HARING
ON FOLLOWING UP AND DISCOVERING NEW HEROES

Sometimes people I met weren't my hero when I met them. In Keith Haring's case, part of the reason he was a hero is how I wound up meeting him.

I was in middle school. And for those who don't know, I went to Cranbrook, which Eminem pointed out in *8-Mile* is "a private school." I'm going to skip trying to explain all the nuances around that and my going there. But the important part to this story is that the school was also home to a graduate art school and museum on a campus designed largely by Saarinen. Yeah. It had an outsized influence on the art world and therefore attracted and hosted an outsized scale of artists. (I met Yoko Ono there once, too, as she was doing an installation.)

Keith Haring was invited to paint a mural. The museum gave him a room and two days. Haring came and painted. And painted. Frenetic colors and black line art. When he got to the end of a color, he nailed the brushes to the wall.

The thing was, the mural would be painted over a month later. Like, that was the plan.

But while he was painting, I got to go watch.

I didn't know much about him going in. But was immediately drawn to his art. The poster from this exhibit hung in my bedroom along with one from his Pop Shop. I wore a Haring sweatshirt apparently too often in high school. I read books, and attended all kinds of his gallery and museum shows, including taking my kids back to Cranbrook when they celebrated the 30th anniversary of his painting with a special show.

My art class was one of a rotation of kids who were able to be there while he worked. We watched him paint. And just wandered around taking it all in. And then he painted on us. And for us. Signing and drawing on sweatshirts, or shoes or whatever people handed him. I didn't have anything, sadly. But he gave us pins, too. So I have a radiant baby he handed me. He even designed the cover of the yearbook for the high school that year.

Meeting my Heroes has some recurring themes. One of them is artists giving back, or somehow connecting with their communities – of place, of fans.

The Cranbrook Art Academy later celebrated Keith Haring's time there by recreating (again, temporarily) part of his work. I was lucky to be able to take my kids.

It's not nearly the same, but it's one of the reasons I liked doing Career Day at my kids' school. I have had an amazing job and career that has let me be me and encouraged curiosity. I've gotten to meet my heroes. I like telling these stories, clearly. But I also like the idea that heroes should be people you want to meet, and that many are people you can meet.

I'll never forget watching him paint. I'll also never really forgive myself for not going back that night to go hear him speak for free. One shouldn't pass up chances like that.

Haring believed that art is for everyone. He created as much as he could in his all-too-short life. He did it because it's what he loved doing. Watching him paint, you could see him embracing the joy of spontaneity.

Mrs. Shaw, the art teacher who took us to see Haring, would attest that art is not really my strong suit. But a lifetime of art education has taught me that it's also important to appreciate good art and be inspired by it in whatever it is you choose to do.

Side note: It was a transitional piece for Haring, a darker view of the world than previous works. Of the piece, Haring wrote:

"A lot of the things that I went through were temporary things. I knew when I was asked to do the piece here (at Cranbrook) that that was the situation. If I didn't want to do it, I would have said no at that point. After I did it, my first reaction when I see it is that it's one of the best drawings that I've ever done. To date. When I was finished I already missed it. I'm going to leave tomorrow and not see it again, ever. I did as much as I could to photograph it because photographs save it forever... So in a way it's like a sacrificial thing, but it also adds to the whole energy of doing the piece."

ERNIE HARWELL
ON BASEBALL AND SOLID STORIES, WELL-TOLD.

| *Ernie Appreciation Day*

My grandfather, B, took my family and me to my first baseball game. It was June, 1981 at Tiger Stadium. A foul ball came right at us, and even though I had my glove, I missed catching it and it wedged itself between the seat and the leg of the man behind me. He didn't even try to catch it, but the ball was his. I was so sad, and B was probably disappointed in me.

I'm sure Ernie Harwell had something to say about it on the radio. He was the long, long, longtime radio broadcaster for the Tigers.

I met Ernie Harwell at Comerica Park with a friend and fellow Tigers fan. He was signing books, including my copy. It was quite a day.

I'd listened to him my entire life, calling Tigers' games on AM 760, WJR. His voice was the perfect southern drawl. He knew everything about the game, and had witnessed much of it personally over the course of his decades-long career. I have some recordings and sometimes in summer I'll put on an old game because no one ever called them the way he did. I was ruined. It was his voice I listened to, on an AM-only radio I carried in my bike basket as I rode around the neighborhood. I remember stopping in the driveway as he called the final out of Jack Morris' no-hitter early in the amazing, magical 1984 season. Later, I would sneak an earbud up my sleeve so I could listen to him during Doc's Latin class as he opened Spring Training each year with a verse from the Bible's Song of Solomon about the voice of the turtle. I would, still later, read that Psalm at my sister's wedding, and she at mine.

I remember watching him in the booth at old Tiger Stadium. I was at Comerica Park in 2002 when they honored him after his retirement, and gave out his bobbleheads. He's the only broadcaster ever traded for a player, Cliff Dapper, and they even had Dapper at the park that day. It was the first time they had ever met!

Ernie certainly had a role in my love for baseball. He took a game I was already falling in love with and wrapped it with a thing I loved even more: stories, well-told.

Ernie showed how stories, spun delicately with just the right amount of detail, make everything better. They pass the time. They fill the gaps and the silence — stretching to fill the space, or staying contained within needed borders. His stories were always the right size to squeeze between pitches or cover the length of a drawn-out inning. They need never get old and, in a way, neither did he. His incredible career also showed that it's possible to do the same thing, more or less, every day of your working life — if you love it. It's possible to do what you love, and be loved. It's important to know your history and the players behind it and weave it into the things you're passionate about today.

Ernie even had something to say about heroes from the perspective of someone who had called them all. "Baseball is a spirited race of man against man, reflex against reflex. A game of inches. Every skill is measured. Every heroic, every failing is seen and cheered, or booed. And then becomes a statistic."

Like every hero eventually, he is now remembered by his stories: those he told and those he starred in.

OK, one last story about Ernie and about me: When Ernie died, my friend Sean was working for the Congressman who represented the district that included Wrigley Field and he made me an incredible offer: "Do you want to write a eulogy for Ernie Harwell for Quigley to give." Um, yes. Yes, I would.

Here it is, direct from the Congressional Record. You can google it!

HON. MIKE QUIGLEY of Illinois in the House of Representatives Monday, May 24, 2010

Mr. QUIGLEY. Madam Speaker, in Ernie Harwell's famous definition of baseball, he wrote that it was "just a game, as simple as a ball and bat; yet as complex as the American spirit it symbolizes." There was nothing complex, however, about what one of baseball's most iconic broadcasters meant to us all. Ernie lent his voice to one of America's deepest loves for more than 50 years, most of them calling games for his beloved Detroit Tigers. He passed away a few short weeks ago at the age of 92.

Ernie brought Tiger Stadium into Michigan living rooms from Hamtramck to Bloomfield, and made the old ballpark at the corner of Michigan and Trumbull feel like a neighborhood sandlot. He'd call out the hometowns of fans who caught foul balls as if he knew all 35,000 of them by name. The beauty of his commentary was in its understated grace--simple, earnest, and full of insight. Ernie was the rare broadcaster who made you feel like you were in the stadium. He'd tell you the score at least once a minute, but never fell victim to the need to hear himself speak. A silence filled with the hum of the crowd and the call of a vendor was almost as important to his broadcast style as the vignettes from every era of the game that peppered his play-by-play.

For Ernie's faithful listeners spring was a time of hope and rebirth, as he welcomed four decades of spring training seasons with a familiar Psalm: "For, lo, the winter is past, the rain is over and gone; the flowers appear on the earth; the time of the singing of birds is come, and the voice of the turtle is heard in our land." It is the kind of hope we can all relate to, especially fans of a certain team in my district who believe that every year might just be "next year."

When Ernie retired from broadcasting in a moving on-field ceremony in 2002, he told us "rather than say good-bye, please allow me to say thank you." Today, it's our turn. Thank you, Ernie, for all the memories. You will be missed.

MR. T
ON HAVING PLANS
AND LOVING IT WHEN
THEY COME TOGETHER

I didn't have a lot of heroes, that I remember, when I was growing up. I certainly didn't consider "super heroes" to be my heroes. Looking back, I'm not sure why. Maybe because they weren't real and their powers were impossible, no matter how much we all wanted to fly. Maybe it was because the things that made them heroes, like massive strength, were traits I would never begin to possess. Not sure.

But I have rarely, if ever, been disappointed in efforts to try to impress my younger selves. I've had that opportunity a few times. These next few chapters will tell those stories:

One hero I remember was Hannibal Smith, the leader of the A-Team. *The A-Team* was a TV show that was big when I was in 4th grade. It aired on Tuesday nights and on Wednesdays we would all talk about it at school. It was about a group of former war heroes who had been falsely accused of some crimes. The police wanted to arrest them, so they were always on the run. But they would help people solve their problems, especially if they were being bullied. The A-Team would show up, build a crazy contraption and fight off the bad guys just in time, before the police showed up. Hannibal would create these elaborate scenarios to trick the bad guys. He'd get all excited and caught up in the preparation and his teammates, like B.A. (Bad Attitude)

Baracus would say, "Watch out, man, he's on the jazz," which basically meant that he was embracing his passion for helping others. Everything would usually go haywire but work out in the end because he had such a great team working behind and with him.

At the end of each episode Hannibal would turn to the rest of the A-Team and say, "I love it when a plan comes together."

Mr. T and the kids (me included, I am 10 in this photo)

That's the part I liked. So much in life works out better when you have a plan. You need to think things through. More importantly, you need to have contingencies for when your initial plot doesn't go as you thought it would. Get wrapped up in it. Soak in the jazz. But also have a plan B. Having a plan C doesn't hurt either. Importantly, when you have done the work of planning, you're in way better shape to vamp when the plans all fall apart, as they often did on the A-Team.

I never met Hannibal, or the actor who played him, George Peppard.

I mentioned another character from the A-Team, B.A. Baracus. He was a big, strong intimidating guy with a mohawk and tons of gold chains around his neck. Like Hannibal, he had a number of catch-phrases like, "I pity the fool," and "quit your jibba jabber." Yes, I'm talking about Mr. T.

So you can imagine my excitement when he came to my block to film the pilot for *I Pity the Tool*, his short-lived DIY home improvement show. Andrew was off at Grandpa's house with his mom, but the rest of us waited patiently for Mr. T to be done shooting so that we could go meet one of Dad's heroes.

His producers were encouraging and offered hints on when he would be free. Eventually the time came and we headed up the block. I heard him talking to one of the crew members as we approached. "It's not an act, man. I'm really like this." And then he said something that his "character" B.A. often said: "I do this for the kids."

He took his time. He gave us Pocket Mr. T toys that my kids love to pull out because Mr. T can get away with telling dad to "Shut Up! Fool!" even if they can't. He took pictures and chatted.

I can't say for sure if B.A. was based on the kindness of Mr. T, or if Mr. T came to be based on the kindness of B.A.

Regardless, he showed us to always be yourself, whoever you are. To be good to other people, stand up for yourself, stand up for others, and support your teammates, even if, and perhaps especially if, they're on the jazz.

All of that is essential to help make those plans come together.

Younger Me had a lot of limits in his world. So I like to do him a solid when I can. And remind myself of how I got to be who I am now. All the versions of me along the way. Maybe I'm trying to be his hero? Maybe trying to validate his choices.

And yes, I have both a Hannibal action figure and a Lego A-Team van with Mr. T on my desk.

Of course I think now about my kids, too. What will they be like at various stages? Who will they look up to and why? Will they get to meet their heroes too?

It's just a shame that not everyone's heroes get to be on the A-Team.

Or do they....

BOY GEORGE

ON THE COMPLICATION OF IDENTITY AND TIME

There are any number of reasons why I liked Culture Club. First and foremost, their songs were good '80s pop that has stood the test of time. Which is not to say it's timeless. It's very '80s. But then again so am I. *Colour by Numbers* dropped in the magical year of 1984. The Tigers won the World Series going wire to wire in first place. *The A-Team* was on every Tuesday night as I recall. And laying on the living room floor listening to Casey Kasem was non-stop hits. "*Thriller*". "*Jump.*" "*Purple Rain.*" The Replacements. And this guy named Boy who dressed not just like a girl but like Cyndi Lauper at that. She was big that year too. He wore bigger hats though.

So there was this curiosity about him. Dee Snider was around in this era. David Bowie had had his *Man who Sold the World* days and was now one of the best dressed and most dapper gentlemen in rock. Was Boy George gay? No one was really gay to a 10-year-old in the suburbs in the '80s. Tipper Gore and Reagan were leading social voices of the day, after all. Boy George was unusually daring and flamboyant but still didn't quite come out and say what was in hindsight rather obvious. Or maybe he did. It's not like you could ask Google at the time.

I didn't know what to make of him. Or if I should even make

anything of him. And it's hard to make sense of what I did or might have thought then from the perspective of today. Or from the perspective of a young pre-adolescent who had his gender roles questioned and challenged by the school bullies.

I especially loved that he was on an episode of the A-team! And that he sang a lot of great songs. Did I respect that he just was, at least mostly, who he was? Maybe?

Meeting Boy George as an adult was entirely about impressing younger me. When Culture Club reunited I was able to interview Roy Hay and Jon Moss for Addicted to Noise. I parlayed that into a photo pass and after show when they came through. Howard Jones was on the same bill and I was pretty excited about that too.

Back stage milling around I chatted with other fans and industry hangers-on. Backstage isn't generally all that exciting, by the way. People waiting around for the stars to maybe show up. Then taking their turns for whatever interaction they are hoping for. I killed time by interviewing Howard Jones' young son.

Backstage I had a weird request. I owned the *Colour by Numbers* album on picture disc. Those were records that weren't just black but had an image on them. I wanted it signed but didn't want them to ruin the record. So I had them sign a piece of acetate that I then layered over it and framed. The manager was a little skeptical because as he pointed out I could put it over anything like "a picture of Hitler" which was of course the example he gave... but he eventually trusted my fandom and helped find the band.

And so a lifetime or two later (if I start counting at 10) I got to meet Boy George. He signed the acetate. He posed for a photo. And we chatted for a moment, about what I honestly don't remember.

But I know that 1984 Me was excited. And I did all I could to soak that in on his behalf. As far as motivations go I think that's a pretty good one. Meet the heroes you had at all points of your life.

Though do the work to evaluate how heroic they still are. Boy George probably made a lot of kids like me, and not really like me, feel like they could be just a little more of whoever they were. No matter what they wore or listened to.

Boy George and me, in my boyhood

COUNT SCARY
ON THE HEROES WHO LIVE NEXT DOOR

Perhaps one of the first heroes I met was literally the hero next door.

I know it's hard to imagine now, but when I was growing up if you wanted to listen to a song, you had to own a record (or tape). Or you could call a radio station that played that type of music and request that they play your song, which they might do, but probably wouldn't.

That's what I spent a lot of the money I'd earn mowing our lawn on: music: from Harmony House, Sam's Jams, Repeat the Beat and other local record stores.

Growing up I lived next door to Tom and Joan Sankovich. They were a nice couple, with a cute dog named Dooley. I would walk him sometimes. Tom was better known as Tom Ryan, which was his DJ name. He was half of a long-running morning show team with Dick Purtan on CKLW and WMOC, which broadcast out of Windsor, Ontario, Canada. Every morning Tom would get up before the sun and drive his Corvette over the border, slowing slightly and waving at the customs agents who all knew him well.

He also had another name, that came with another car. He was Count Scary. Count Scary was the cool, kooky host of horror movies on a local TV station around Halloween, and a character on Tom's radio show. Kind of a local celebrity. He did commercials, had a couple of songs on the radio and even had his own fan club, of which I was of course a member.

The Scary Mobile in the Count's driveway.

Now you can find Count Scary videos on YouTube. And there are some cool interviews and stories about Tom Ryan, where I learned a lot about my former neighbor.

He was also a super nice guy. He was always giving me Count Scary swag. Even asked my opinion on if he should change out his trademark Converse for a new pair of Nikes. (I said he should stick with the original kicks, and he did.)

When they moved, he left me an amazing present: two boxes of 45 rpm records, otherwise known as singles. Each record had two songs on it and the artists were a lot of names I knew, and have tried to teach my kids as part of their musical education: The Beatles, Little Richard, Elvis, the Temptations, the Four Tops, Jan and Dean and The Beach Boys. It was a rich collation of rocknroll history. I would listen to them one-by-one on my little record player in my room, or the stereo in the living room. I learned a lot by listening to those songs by the bands I knew and by the bands I didn't know.

Because he was a DJ, he got a lot of special records, too, such as the first Beatles single released in the U.S.: "My Bonnie" and "When the Saints go Marching in," performed with the Tony Sheridan Orchestra. There were also weird records and public service announcements.

It was a pretty insignificant thing for him to give away — he had no shortage of other records, but for me it was a treasure, and one I still keep in my basement.

I had a chance to thank him for that many years later. My dad and I were shopping for a tool chest for my first house at one of the big box hardware stores. I saw Mr. Ryan at the check-out and called him by his birth name which confused him. He said he hadn't used that name in ages. I'm glad I got to share how much that collection meant to me, and how much that legacy of great songs still does. I think he was happy to hear that, too.

Being thoughtful is amazing. But even a little off-handed generosity can go a long way.

MOJO NIXON AND DEBBIE GIBSON

ON MEETING THE PARENTS OF A BIGFOOT BABY

When I was in high school I would often fall asleep listening to the local high school radio station. It played a lot of artists that didn't get much other airtime like Camper Van Beethoven, the Dead Milkmen and Mojo Nixon. WBFH also went to bed at the same time I did, with an FCC-mandated sign-off message at 10pm sharp.

I really enjoyed the cleverness and humor in the lyrics of all three of those bands. One of Mojo's best-known songs was a tabloid spoof about how pop singer Debbie Gibson "was pregnant with [his] two-headed love child, a bigfoot baby all covered in fur now."

I'm proud to say that I'm one of probably very few people who met both parents of that baby Yeti.

I met the Dead Milkmen when I was in high school at a record signing my mom, amazingly enough, pulled me out of school early to go to. Later, I would shoot Camper Van Beethoven as House Photographer for Metro. But I didn't meet Mojo until 2019. He wasn't touring much anymore, but a local brewery made a beer in his honor and got Mojo to come out and play at a launch party. The show was great fun and I enjoyed every moment and remembered way too many lyrics than I should have. I caught up with him before the show for a quick selfie and hello.

| This book has Mojo Nixon

I've tried to pass along my love of Mojo to my kids and was quite proud of a moment where I was driving past an oddly landlocked boat parked in front of a building and asked, "who needs a boat." My son replied, "ELVIS!"

My work as a parent was done. I can leave the building.

Meeting Debbie Gibson was fun, too. The Cubs would sometimes have nostalgia music artists come throw out a first pitch and sing the seventh-inning stretch as part of a promotion like "70s night" or "80s night." And having musicians there made it a music story, so I pitched my editors at Billboard.com and talked them into letting me cover these important music events.

The first year was Journey for '70s night. I was amazed that the photo pass issued by the Cubs granted me full press privileges, not just for the performance. So twice I got to shoot some of the game from the field press boxes. I could walk between the first and third base boxes ON THE FIELD during the game. I hung out upstairs in the press box. One of those times I found Max from Poi Dog, who runs some of the scoreboards at Wrigley (he got a World Series ring!). Max was bemused to find me in his third office (having seen me countless times in his other two, Poi's stage and Metro, where he was a bartender and I was House Photogra-

MEETING MY HEROES

pher). He let me punch Derrick Lee's uniform number into the original score board when he came up to bat!

| Debbie Gibson singing the 7th inning stretch.

Anyway, shooting the Cubs is how I found myself in the broadcast booth as first Journey (during the same week I shot Robin Williams getting a lifetime achievement award, as well as shows by Madonna and KISS!) and a year later Debbie Gibson sang the seventh-inning stretch. I also interviewed Debbie and took a bunch of photos of her.

Several funny things came of all of this:

One, people really watch the Cubs on TV. All kinds of random friends called or emailed the next day: "DID I SEE YOU ON TV????"

Two, someone made a fake Debbie Gibson baseball card using one of my photos.

And most amusingly, Debbie's manager (her mom) tracked me down the next day and said Debbie wanted to call me because she had a couple follow-up thoughts for our interviews. I chatted my friends, "Debbie Gibson is trying to get my digits!" And she was!

. . .

Fourteen-year-old Me, listening to WBFH in my room after bedtime, would have found this all HILARIOUS and also unbelievable.

Me (in the backwards Cubs hat) shooting the Cubs

As with Boy George, or Mr. T., whenever I do things to amuse my younger self, my current self does not regret it. But also, in life it's important to always work the angles. I turned a baseball story into a music story and because of that, I got to stand on Wrigley Field without getting arrested.

MEETING MY HEROES

ORSON SCOTT CARD
ON THE COMPLICATED PEOPLE WHO MAKE COMPLICATED ART

When I was just out of college and living near Belmont and Sheffield, I happened to live near the city's (and, really, one of the nation's) best sci-fi book stores, The Stars our Destination. Besides a fantastic selection and wonderful staff (including Sprite, a friend of my roommate, Jack's), they would from time to time host book signings from some of the best authors of our time. And so I got to meet Orson Scott Card, who wrote one of my favorite books, *Speaker for the Dead*, the sequel to the also-awesome *Ender's Game*. (And yes, that Ender is related to the Ender in Minecraft.)

Reading "Ender's Game," there were a couple of concepts I have taken with me over the years. One is that "the enemy's gate is down," which basically means you need to orient whatever you're doing so that the goal is in front of you and your gravity will carry you forward, toward it. It can be as simple as turning a map as you travel. Or more intricate on a long-term project. Another was about winning wars, not battles. Mostly, that the world is complicated, as are people's motivations, and you need to try to stay human and empathetic as you go.

Speaker for the Dead is about the complicated legacies of people and the value in telling the truth, even if it's a hard truth. That idea has gotten messed up over the years as people talk about being "real," when really they mean honest or even cruel without that empathy.

I shared these books with my dad, who also liked them a lot. Now I'm sharing (his copies) with my kids.

At the book signing, I picked up a copy of *Ender's Game* for my cousin, Ted and got *Ender's Shadow*, one of the sequels, for myself. But while I was in line, the kid in front of me challenged Card on his beliefs about LGBTQ people. I think he called Card a homophobe.

Card pushed back, hard. It was clear he'd heard this all before and didn't have much patience for it. He said some comments he'd made ages ago had been taken out of context and he tried to explain how he really felt.

Lesson one is it's OK to challenge your heroes (maybe politely but firmly). Lesson two is to hear out your critics and respond to them if you think it's worth it. Sometimes it's not. Sometimes you're not going to change someone's mind and it can be exhausting to keep trying.

Card signed my copy of *Ender's Shadow* with his amazingly artful signature. He wrote, "Matt, in the light, how can shadows hide?"

Unfortunately, Card's shadows came out as more and more light was shone on them.

This was before "cancel culture" became a thing. The bigger lesson is that people can make good art, even if they're not great humans. Card really seems to be not the best human. He's made that more and more clear in the years since I saw him at a book signing, which was the first I'd heard of it. This Wired story, headlined "Orson Scott Card: Mentor, Friend, Bigot," does a solid job of laying out how complex life can be.

There are a lot of philosophies about what to do with artists who aren't great humans. Some take a zero-tolerance policy. Some consider how important they are to the history of their craft. In some cases, like Bill Cosby or Michael Jackson, you can't really tell the story of comedy or pop music without them. I sometimes think about it in terms of: "does knowing about the artist change how you see the art?" Gary Glitter, I'm looking at you.

So, as you read Card's works — or anyone's for that matter — it's good to keep in mind the ideologies of the person behind it, when you know what they are. Sometimes they're obvious. Sometimes they're subtle. Sometimes you don't even know from reading it. JK Rowling, I'm looking at you, too.

But it's all about becoming critical readers and thinkers, which are more important skills than ever these days.

And despite all of his shortcomings, *Ender's Game* and *Speaker for the Dead* are still amazing books.

RICKEY HENDERSON
ON THE COMPLICATED PEOPLE WHO MAKE COMPLICATED ART

Rickey Henderson was a Hall of Fame baseball player, born on Christmas Day in Chicago in the back seat of an Oldsmobile that didn't get to the hospital in time.

Rickey was what's called a lead-off hitter, meaning Rickey was the first guy in the batting order. I would argue that Rickey was the absolute best player ever at doing the thing he was paid to do. Rickey's job was to get on base, and run really fast when the guys after him in the batting order got hits, so that he could score runs and give his team an early lead. Rickey is the all-time leader in: lead-off homers, unintentional walks (a way to get on base), stolen bases (a way to get closer to scoring) and runs scored. So Rickey basically holds the all-time records in every facet of his job. As Rickey once told a sports writer, "If you could split him in two, you'd have two Hall of Famers."

Rickey got a lot of flak for a thing he said once about how he was the greatest. The context was maybe the problem. But he wasn't wrong. He actually was. And I think it should be OK to say that.

Rickey often referred to himself in the third person, like when Rickey called a baseball team to talk about a contract. He didn't have an agent, like most players. Instead he called up and said, "This is Rickey, representing Rickey." Rickey was a little quirky.

Rickey played left field, which is the position in baseball that gets the least action and so he'd get bored and kick the grass, turn around with his back to the plate and stare into space. Yet, he was still an amazing outfielder and even one of the best, in that he was one of the all-time leaders in outfield putouts. Rickey knew how to play.

Rickey played for a lot of teams, but never on a team I rooted for. So I liked to go see him play against teams I did, and later against the White Sox. I'd sit out by left field and root for Rickey. Lots of people also liked to heckle Rickey, again because he didn't always seem focused on his job.

Pam and I once took a trip to New Jersey to see David Bowie and the Polyphonic Spree in concert. Somehow I talked her into also seeing a Newark Bears game. It was kind of like going to the Chicago Dogs — fun, but not the best baseball. Rickey was playing out his final games, not major league material anymore, but not ready to give up the game he loved, either.

I brought my 1980 Topps Henderson rookie card in a little plastic sleeve, hoping that in the informal setting of this tiny minor-league park I might get him to sign it. I had a Sharpie just in case. Always have a Sharpie. Always.

Anyway, around the 7th inning I noticed Rickey making his way for the locker room. I rushed off toward the tunnel, card in hand, and hopes on high. I caught him as he ducked in and caught his attention. "Rickey," I shouted, "I came here from Chicago just to see you play, will you sign!" and lowered my card toward him. I might have exaggerated slightly, in that I really came to see Bowie, but Rickey, too.

Rickey looked up at me, kind of nervously and looked around. I realized he was ducking out and didn't want to get busted by his manager. "Sorry, man," he said, "Rickey's gotta go."

And the stolen base leader didn't run, but kind of slinked away.

I can't say I was disappointed. Because that moment didn't take away from a lifetime of his being a hero. He wasn't a jerk about it. Sometimes your heroes can fulfill your dreams, sure. If they don't, it doesn't mean they aren't still your heroes, or shouldn't be. It just means that they have to go do some hero stuff somewhere else. Like, right now. Even if that hero stuff is just slipping away before their boss catches them.

Rickey Henderson with the Newark Bears. Sir Speedy, indeed.

MEETING MY HEROES

MITCH ALBOM
ON FINDING THE PATH TO YOUR PATH

My parents used to leave the *Detroit Free Press* on the kitchen table. Sometimes just lying there because that's where papers went when they came in the house. Sometimes open to something they wanted me to read. Kids will read most anything you leave out while they're eating breakfast, it seems.

I read through most of the paper while I had my cereal or yogurt in the mornings. But I loved reading about the Tigers, so I'd look at the sports and, of course, the comics. I'd read Dave Barry's essays too.

I also just loved good writing and there were few, if any, better newspaper writers in Detroit at that time than Mitch Albom. He was first and foremost a sports writer. But he also had a column where he could clearly write about most anything he wanted to. He told great stories and he told them well. About the biggest athletes of the time and also more human and personal pieces.

One piece that stuck with me was about how gymnastics was essentially a form of abuse. He wrote:

"I love the sport of women's gymnastics, it is breathtaking, like dance, the purest command of the human body. But I defy anyone to attend an Olympic gymnastics competition — at least anyone who loves children — and not walk out terribly upset."

Not far from where he wrote this, even more abuse was

happening in this sport. But most of us didn't know that at the time.

But what I appreciated was that he showed you could be a journalist and write about something non-serious like sports and also make it serious. This was a pretty extreme example, but throughout his writing he tackled bigger topics than the sports themselves. Or he told the personal stories within the broader context of sports. He wrote about whatever he wanted to, and he did it well.

Despite applying to journalism schools, I wasn't sure I actually wanted to be a journalist. But I was pretty sure that if I did, I wasn't going to do Pulitzer-winning investigative reporting. Or be a war correspondent. That's just not what I wanted. But could I write about music the way Mitch Albom wrote about sports? Maybe? Did I want to write like Hunter S. Thompson? Uh huh. Reading the best journalism of Rolling Stone, or the interviews of Playboy (it's a book with no illustrations) helped, too.

Albom was also into music. He was part of a band made up of authors called the Rock Bottom Remainders. Over the years it also included Stephen King, Amy Tan, Dave Barry, Matt Groening and more. Sometimes they even had actual musicians like legendary guitarist for the Byrds, Roger McGuinn. They would perform to raise money for charity, because heroes give back.

In 2004, they played a show at Chicago's House of Blues. The band asked if they could use my photos on its site. Since their performances were for charity, I donated my time, too. But then they asked if I would come early and shoot a band portrait! Which meant I was around for sound check and got to meet some of them, including Mitch. I had him sign one of his books for me, and told him a little bit about how he was an inspiration and why. They are still using my photos on their site, and I had shots posted on Dave Barry's blog for a while, which was quite a thrill as I was a fan of his, too. I was credited as "actual photographer Matt Carmichael."

MEETING MY HEROES

Mitch Albom and the Rock Bottom Remainders

I have been in a position to meet so many of my heroes, like Mitch Albom, because I am a journalist – so it was meta to get to thank him for helping me grapple with getting to journalism. By the time I met him, he had inspired Younger Me to grow into Then-Current Me and both Mes were thrilled by the encounter.

College is about connections, and friends and all the things you learn outside the classroom. How I got from journalism school to actual journalism is quite a story. So let's take a little detour just off campus.

STEVE YAHN
ON BUILDING, NOT BURNING, BRIDGES

The single moment that most changed my life took place on a street corner off-campus from Northwestern on a random afternoon, much like any other.

It's a moment that would never have taken place if I hadn't first had that chance conversation with Dr. Welch about applying for editor-in-chief. Or if Doc hadn't written that letter to Northwestern. Or if my friend and dorm neighbor Freddie hadn't suggested I run for President of Willard. But those things happened and they set me up for this moment.

I was standing with Andy Carvin. Andy had graduated and was visiting from D.C. where he lived. He had previously lived in the late, great Willard room 121 years before me. We were waiting for Chris Crone (of which the same could be said) who worked near this corner. If I had to guess we were planning to go to My Bar for a litre of Pilsner Urquell. He was squinting at everyone who walked by because he wasn't wearing his glasses. He squinted at someone he thought might be Chris but turned out to be another recent grad who was visiting from New York, a guy named David Levin.

So if you're following, I'm on a corner a ways from campus. It's not a highly trafficked area to start with. I'm standing with someone from out of town and someone else from out of town walks by and amazingly enough, these two guys know each other pretty well. How's that for coincidence and chance?

We get to talking, Andy introduces me and says I'm a journalism major interested in this new thing called the Internet. David Levin works at Advertising Age and says, "Oh, in that case you should talk to my editor, Scott Donaton."

Amazingly, he follows through and introduces me to Scott. It was early spring and all the college kids were trying to hook up their summer internships so the timing was great.

Scott called my room to set up an interview. I was down the hall but a friend of my roommate's answered the phone: "Matt and Jon's love shack," she said.

Thankfully, Scott didn't hold that against me. Nor did he give up on me when I spilled my drink on myself during our lunch interview.

Instead, he took me back to the office to meet the Editor of *AdAge*, Steve Yahn. And here's where it gets weird.

I'm standing, nervous, outside the door to the office. Scott is inside talking to Steve, "I've got this intern candidate I'd like you to meet..."

I hear Yahn inside. He's a little manic and excited. "Well that's great, bring his ass in here, we'll show him how the hell we do things around here..." And as he says this I come into view and he snaps into a different persona mid-sentence. "Hey, Steve Yahn," he said, offering his hand to shake, "Great to meet you."

We sit down at the table in his office and as we talk, Scott mentions that I have my own web site which was incredibly uncommon at that moment in time, and basically why they were interested in hiring me. *AdAge* itself barely had a web site at the time.

Yahn asked me what it was about, and I was a little embarrassed. I wanted to say it was about something serious and lofty like journalism ethics, or politics or something. But I told the truth. It was about Lou Reed and the Velvet Underground.

Yahn slapped both hands on the desk, pushed back and stood

up. "LOU REED! I saw the Velvets back in '66 at the Dom!" he yelled, now manic again. I couldn't have been more shocked and honestly more jealous. I can think of few concerts I would have wanted to see more. But then we talked Lou Reed for a bit.

I was hired for the internship.

But here was a quintessential case of chance and being prepared to take advantage of it – mixed with a dash of privilege to get passed to the top of the list, if there was a list. I honestly don't remember if this internship even existed before it was offered to me.

The internship was not easy, but I liked the people and Yahn put me on retainer ($100 a week of basically free money. That was a TON of money) my senior year so he could call me up and ask me questions whenever he wanted to. I wrote pieces for *AdAge* from time to time, which was incredible experience for a college kid. Most importantly, I didn't burn any bridges, which I could have if I hadn't stuck it out for the internship, or had ended it poorly.

However, it's good that bridge was still there. In the very short term because when Steve was no longer with Crain he and I worked on a few Web projects together. Steve would hang out in my dorm room because I had a network connection instead of dial-up. Or we would meet at a bar. We helped build what I think was the first-ever live auction on the Internet with Leslie Hindman as our client. True story. Every last word. He was a great mentor, a fun guy to have a beer with, and a man of many talents. I quite literally wouldn't be where I am today without him.

And in the longer term, it was good because eventually *AdAge* hired me for my first full-time job and I would have a crazy ride through the dotcom boom right up until 2000 when my job went to New York and I decided to stay in Chicago, which had become home. More on that story later.

As an aside, remember that thing I was saying in the Dr. Welch story about teachers and how they can nudge you with their belief or push you with their lack of faith?

My freshmen year advisor at Medill was a professor named Mary Ann Weston. She'd won a Pulitzer Prize for covering the 1967 race riots in Detroit.

She never thought I would amount to much of anything because, by my first week of school, I didn't know what I wanted to do and I certainly didn't plan to be a hard-nosed reporter like she had been. Mad respect for those who are, but that's not what I wanted to do with my degree (as alluded to in the Mitch Albom story...).

Anyway, I ran into her right at the end of my senior year on the steps of Fisk Hall, home of the journalism school. She asked me what I was doing after graduation. The look on her face when I told her that I had an "editor" job at a well-known, well-respected publication was worth every bit of work I put in at Northwestern. Proving her wrong was a great feeling. There are a lot of ways to motivate yourself. Pettiness can be one of them. Your mileage may vary, but trust me, it can work.

But back to *AdAge*, I still didn't burn any bridges (despite being asked point-blank if I wanted to during my exit interview?!?) when I left that full-time role. Which was good, because a few years later its sibling publication *Crain's Chicago* would hire me back into the company and then I'd move back to *AdAge* itself and then back to *Crain's Chicago*.

I've never held a job that someone held before, nor have I ever been replaced exactly. I've chosen my own adventure and made my own career path. But I've also always wound up working in some way with the people from jobs I've left, or been hired back outright.

You never know when you might need something on the side of the river you left behind. Always leave the bridges there, so you can scramble back to safety if you need.

That's two big lessons in one big story. Each is important on its own, and together they'll set you on the right road, help you blaze your path, and give you a way out if you should need it.

PART FOUR
WORDS AND MUSIC
ON THE WRITERS, MUSICIANS AND CREATORS WHO INSPIRED ME TO CREATE, TOO

JOHN RICHARDS
ON THE POWER OF MUSIC AND CONNECTION, OF COMMUNITY AND RADIO

Three generations of my family have been college and/or high school DJs, myself and my wife included. Music – and radio – are important to us. If my family has a mutual hero, it's John Richards.

KEXP, 90.3 Seattle, was one of the first stations to stream all its content. It's listener-supported radio. It's all music. And it's programmed in real time by humans. The morning show is spun by a DJ named John Richards whose show is part Gen-X warm blanket comfort food nostalgia, part new music discovery and part therapy session. He can weave a set from Mozart to punk rock to hip hop in a way that really only a human can make work. Wait, did I just hear the Muppets? Was that really Ministry? Before 8am?!?

KEXP has become a staple for my family, who have now listened for nearly half or literally all of their lives, depending. We hear favorites and learn about new bands. We listen to the Friday song. We invented – and John blessed on-air – Beastie Boys Thursday. John gave an on-air nod to my dad after he spun an amazing set I heard while driving back from my dad's funeral. Lizzo to Deee-Lite to "O-o-h Child" from the Five Stairsteps. Where else on the dial will you hear that?

We've connected on social media, too, including a funny

discussion on Twitter about my Brubeck near-meeting and the awkwardness of bathroom encounters.

We support the station, and we enjoy the occasional shout-outs for graduations, or birthdays. It's interwoven with our rituals.

Humans have a need to connect with and through music. KEXP, and John Richards' show in particular, has three mantras: "Music matters," "Music heals," and, most powerfully, "You are not alone." I keep a KEXP pin with that saying on my desk. Arguably, this connection between music and mental health has always existed. For many, myself included, it crystalized during the pandemic when music helped keep me sane-ish. Ipsos research shows that mental health is a growing part of our wellness conversations. The first time I met John, it was over Zoom as I interviewed him for WTF's Music issue. He told me then,

"Music can heal. Music can also gut you. But mostly, music can get you through if you let it."

He went on:

"Music is always going to fill in the words that you don't have for yourself. They're going to sing the songs that are going to tell the story of you. You can't come up with those words. You don't even know how to start. And then you hear a song or a mood in a song and it's able to. It could be Mozart or TV on the Radio's 'Trouble' or the Mountain Goats' 'This Year.' Those songs will fill in that blank. You should be doubling down on your love for music and your need for music in troubled times as you get older. You go to music to get lost and fill in the blanks. At least the people who do. There are plenty who don't, but those are sad people who lead boring lives."

So yes, humans have a need to connect with and through music. And I have a need to connect, too, with my heroes. It's not an exaggeration to say that KEXP was top of the to-do list for all of us as we took a spring break trip to Seattle. And it's no shock that I was hoping we could meet John.

We don't want to be sad people who lead boring lives.

The station's physical space is a community center with a coffee shop and record store in an open common area called the Gathering Space. Folks come, hang out, take Zoom calls, meet their Realtor or attorney or whatever other third space thing needs to happen. The main DJ booth has windows on two sides overlooking the space. Live performances are open to the public and free and take place all the time.

So we got up, headed out and went to watch John. My daughter thought it was like a weird zoo experience. My son stood by the window watching John work, and dance and rock out. There are a lot of buttons and screens to make radio work now.

While we were standing there, the facilities manager found us and gave us a quick tour of the observation room for the live space, where you can watch the famous YouTube live shows being recorded. A band was setting up to be filmed later. The manager was really nice, and told us about the reclaimed clam wood on the side of the DJ booth with bore holes from the clams.

And just as John's set wrapped up, John's producer Owen popped out at the end of a donor tour. He saw us and put together that we were the family who had emailed earlier in the morning. He said the magic words: "Want to come meet John and see the booth?"

When we entered, John said he saw my son outside watching just like his son Henry would have, and he had to invite us in.

The rest is a little blurry, as were the photos Owen tried to take on my camera which has a tricky autofocus. So we redid them with my phone, and Owen also took a selfie.

John showed us the booth and all the screens and playlists and spreadsheets of albums (I'd like a copy of his 450 must-listen album list to work on my kids' music curriculum). And was kind and charming and disarming as we all couldn't believe we were there. Owen then gave us a tour of the rest of the station: the library with vinyl going back to their KCMU days with white stickers on the songs that were "too overplayed" to go on their station. Take that REM! He showed us the live space from the other side of the glass. (I saw Aldous Harding perform there pre-pandemic, on a show that was memorable because the soundboard crashed right before the taping. Ooops.) He even showed us the kitchen, which Barry, the facilities manager we had met, had brilliantly decorated with food-themed records.

The kids were so excited, as were their parents. They texted their also-excited friends, which is the ultimate expression of teen meaningfulness.

John carries the burden of his community, this community which he has forged around the music. People post and write and text every day about the grief and sorrow and victories in their lives. Myself included. It's a community John curates around proving every day that we are not alone. But it takes a toll on someone who has his own struggles with anxiety and depression.

If that kind of thing isn't heroic, I don't know what is.

When I interviewed John for WTF we of course talked about the joy of human curation of music. And we went pretty deeply into that connection between music and mental wellness. I asked him about carrying that burden. That discussion didn't make it into the issue so I'm including it here. He seemed genuinely touched that I asked and he told me this about hosting the morning show:

"You are waking a lot of people up, especially in Seattle. They trust you and feel comfortable. I'm glad they do. I don't want them to stop, but yeah, it'll probably shorten my radio career. It'll probably be the thing where I'm like, I think I gotta go take care of John for a while and step away at some point."

I hope that day never comes. I also hope that I'll be understanding if it does. As I said, John and KEXP help keep me sane-ish. I can't wish any less for him.

For all of us: Don't be a sad person. Don't lead a boring life. Be as curious about discovering new music as you are about everything else in life. Rocknroll can save your life. It can change your life. So, for that matter, can jazz. I learned that from another hero.

All you have to do is take the advice of a different Jon. Jon Hendricks.

Because sometimes you meet your heroes. Sometimes you meet other people's heroes. Sometimes, maybe the best times – you get to introduce your kids to their heroes, like John. All of those are important.

And remember: You. Are. Not. Alone.

Meeting KEXP DJ *John Richards* in the DJ booth

EVERCLEAR

ON BEING FRIENDLY BUT NOT BEING FRIENDS

One of the first "rock star" interviews I did was with the band Everclear. While they've gone on to ride the success of a couple '90s albums into a lengthy career, they were just starting to break in 1995. I talked to them before a sold-out show at Metro. I was interviewing Everclear and, as a favor to their publicist, I also sat down with the opener of the three-band bill, Ruth Ruth. In between those sets I caught a little bit of the second band and was quite impressed. I made a note to keep an eye on them and yeah, No Doubt did pretty well, too!

I was still in college, so this was a pretty cool day. I was even repurposing my reporting on a project called "A day in the life of the Internet," in which people from all over the world collaborated on documenting how the Internet was affecting their lives in different ways. Keep in mind this was 1995 or so. The Internet, or at least the Web, was still very young.

I liked their music, and the singer seemed like a guy who had faced a lot in his life and channeled it into, well, art.

Anyway, there's a scene in every movie about rocknroll where they do a montage of a band's first major tour and the managers keep bringing in copies of *Billboard* magazine. *Billboard* publishes charts of how well music is selling and the managers would show off how well their band was moving up the charts toward the goal of having a #1 best-selling hit song.

I was sitting on a tour bus, interviewing the band, when I got to witness this scene in action. The manager hopped on the bus with a *Billboard* in hand and showed them that they had hit the coveted Top 40 and were moving up.

It was an interesting interview. The singer told me I had asked a dumb question (I might disagree), but then complimented the next one I asked. So I learned a bit about the craft of interviewing as I went.

Later, I'd interview that singer, Art Alexakis, again at a solo show at The Fireside Bowl, a bowling alley in Chicago that hosted punk shows. And I ran into him backstage at a show at the United Center, as they continued to gain in popularity. He was the first "rock star" who knew me on sight, which was really exciting.

But that didn't mean we were friends. It's how I started to learn the "professional distance" that journalists have, and fundamentally need to have, with the people they write about. You can't, or at least shouldn't, write about your friends. By extension, you can't let yourself become friends with those you cover. Most bands know this already and aren't really in any hurry to be friends with you either. Heh.

As Jon Hendricks said, you have to listen. And when you do that, more than talk, you learn what you need from the people you're talking to. That's true in interviews and pretty much all of the rest of the time. The point isn't to impress the people you're interviewing with how smart/cool you are. It's to make enough of a connection with them so that they're comfortable telling you, and having you then tell your audience their story. But it's OK to let a bit of your story in too from time to time.

ALANIS MORISETTE
ON PERSISTENCE

Sometimes you hear a record and you just know. Wow, this is full of hits. Alanis Morissette's *Jagged Little Pill* was one of those records for me. I got a promo copy at the magazine I was interning for, *CoverStory*. It was easy to see it would be huge, though I'm not sure anyone would have really guessed how huge. It's one of the best-selling of all time, with over 33 million copies.

I reached out for an interview, hoping to do something in person on her planned visit to Chicago a few weeks later. I figured I had a decent shot as her record had just dropped and no one knew who she was. But that all changed shortly. After quite a bit of back and forth with the publicist, she got too big too fast for our magazine. How big? She became the first artist allowed to break the long-standing unwritten rule that you couldn't be on the cover of *Spin* and *RollingStone* at the same time. She was on the cover of both magazines within weeks.

To add a lot of insult to my injury, the *Spin* interview was conducted right before her Chicago show on her Detroit tour stop. And the guy interviewed her while walking around the campus of my high school. Ugh.

CoverStory was a kind of magazine called a "total market coverage" magazine, which meant it got included with the market fliers and coupons and distributed to every home in a town. So it had a distribution of over 4 million in mostly small and mid-sized cities. I interned there my junior year of college and couldn't have been happier with the assignment. Oddly, I was initially assigned to work for a Crain publication called *Electronic Media* and likely would have been working for someone who eventually became a colleague and a friend, Betsy. I don't remember why I got switched over to *CoverStory* but it was a perfect fit. I got to do a little bit of everything from pitching and writing to editing and proofing. And every Thursday we would pack a disk with the files for the issue and a set of pre-proof pages into Fed-Ex tubes and ship them to our client papers in places like Fond du Lac, Wisconsin. Shipping was an all-hands process, literally. I had to wake up really early to get there and take the purple line downtown on the L to the blue line and take that almost out to O'Hare, then walk or bus a mile from there. Sometimes I got a ride with a classmate who worked there. And often I got a ride home with a friend who was interning nearby that quarter.

| *Alanis, a frenetic blur of energy and emotion at Metro*

Through *CoverStory* I got to build my writing portfolio and interview fun people (though not Alanis). You'll hear a couple more of those stories later. The best part was that I was able to freelance for them when the internship was over. It was my first paid journalism gig, and they paid quite well. I wrote for them all through senior year – one of several jobs I had while trying to balance schoolwork and figuring out what I wanted to do with the rest of my life and some hobbies and hanging out with friends enjoying the last year of college before Adulthood.

But back to Alanis...

While I failed to get the interview, I did get to cover that first Chicago show at Metro. It was sold out and packed and everyone already knew every word of every song. There's nothing like moments like that where you catch an artist just as they break in a venue so small they'll never be able to play it again. I think I still have the set list, too. All 11 songs of it.

I shot the show on both black and white and color film.

So now I had original photos. I looked around and there was basically nothing about Alanis on the Web yet. But since I had my own content, I put up what would be the first Alanis site. I hosted it on the same server as my Lou Reed and Poi Dog Pondering pages on one of the Unix workstations. Then I moved it to a Mac-based web server that I helped administer. But it got so much traffic I eventually needed to move it off-campus (also I was graduating).

Maybe I'll tell some more Alanis web stories later, but let's get to the part where I met her...

It would be almost another decade.

By now I was a pretty established writer and photographer. I was shooting a lot for Billboard.com and WXRT radio and represented by the wire service, Getty Images. I was House Photographer for Metro. And through Pam, I was also House Photographer at the big outdoor amphitheaters, Alpine Valley and what was then the Tweeter Center. We'll talk more about all of that as we go.

I saw Alanis perform several times over the years. Never again at some place as small as Metro. But places like the United Center. And a Yahoo! Music awards show where she performed just a couple of songs, as did Isaac Hayes, Aimee Mann and David Bowie. You might remember that's where I met Martha Stewart the first time. Finally I saw Alanis at the Tweeter Center. After I shot the show I was also asked to do a quick favor for her label, Reprise.

I therefore wound up shooting a bunch of people meeting their hero, too. But we had some down time between groups of folks so I told her some of the story and asked her to sign my original Metro photo pass from a decade earlier.

Alanis had a really interesting career, as a child star and performer. Then she grew up and totally reinvented herself. She took her experiences and turned them into art. Since *Jagged Little Pill* dropped she never had another hit that large, but still put together a decent catalog, reinventing herself a few more times along the way, as a mother and a role model among other new hats she wears.

I, too, am not the Me I was when I first tried to meet her. Nor the Me I was when I finally did meet her. But one thing you learn, as a young journalist, is persistence. And when you hear a hit, jump as fast as you can because others will hear it too.

JOEY RAMONE
ON CONFIDENCE

My son, Andrew, thinks the Ramones are the greatest band ever. Which means he has an important thing in common with Joey Ramone, the group's singer. Joey was also convinced the Ramones were the best band ever. I didn't get to meet Joey in person. We had a phone interview, me at the *AdAge* office where I was interning. Him in a hotel room in Utah somewhere. Shortly after, I saw them on their 1996 farewell tour and took the photo Andrew now has framed in his room.

The interview happened around the dawning of what we know as the Internet and I always asked people about that and questions that seem quaint now, like "Do you have an email address?". He was writing a column for the web-based site I was writing for, Addicted to Noise, but he was not particularly online himself. He said this of the Internet, "It ain't the same world it was when we were growing up. Things are different these days, especially with computers. Everyone is plugged in. You're not left in the dark anymore the way it was back in another time. People are more enlightened. Some people anyway."

That last part was especially prescient all these years later.

What did I learn from him, other than a lot of "kids these days! Get off my lawn!" theories of punk in the mid '90s? Just that you should always believe you're the best at what you do. I mean, why not? Have unwavering faith in yourself and what you're doing. That doesn't mean you shouldn't listen to others, and take criticism, and learn from your mistakes, and, more importantly, acknowledge your mistakes. No, all that is good and should actually strengthen what you do, not weaken it. And it doesn't mean you can't be humble. And strive to get better.

But at the end of the day, you need to be your own best cheerleader. Because while many will wind up on your side if you do things right, not everyone will.

Of course, it's also OK if you're not actually the absolute leader in the field you choose to pursue. That's cool, and that's likely. But be the best You doing the best you can at the thing you love.

And maybe wake up every morning with a "Hey! Ho!Let's Go!"

| *Joey Ramone for Coverstory*

FRANK ORRALL AND THE REST OF THE POI DOGS

ON FAMILY, AND HOME, AND STANDING EXACTLY WHERE YOU'RE SUPPOSED TO BE

I first saw Poi Dog Pondering at a concert on Northwestern's campus called 'Dillo Day (it's on YouTube!). It was an annual outdoor festival on the lakefront right before final exams. The show clearly changed my life. I went right from the show to a Chicago Compact Disc store and picked up "Volo Volo," and later their other two albums out at the time.

I became a fan, and the following summer Poi Dog Pondering was playing at Grant Park on the 4th of July. I was spending the summer on campus and helping edit the "summer" issue of *Art+Performance* by night and working in the campus computing lab by day.

I assigned myself to cover the Poi show and wrote a story. I loved writing it, and I loved how it turned out. That story (see below) would lead to both a longstanding relationship with the band and a longstanding misunderstanding.

First thing's first.

Poi played two shows that 4th of July, 1994, including an after-show at Lounge Ax. Leddie, their percussionist at the time, walked me in because I was underage. They played both as Poi Dog Pondering and as a side-project of theirs called Palm Fabric Orchestra, debuting the CD from that instrumental ensemble. That CD lived in my player all summer.

I met Frank that night, and interviewed him and Susan in the basement.

Once the shows were over, I had a story and a bunch of photos of the band, because I had talked my way into a photo pass despite only having a point-and-shoot Olympus that my parents had bought me years before. It was called a point-and-shoot because that's all you had to do. It was a fully automatic camera. I think I had one roll of black and white film.

But armed with all of this content, and a severe case of fanboy, I started building a Web site. Like most bands, Poi Dog Pondering didn't have a site of its own at that point. This was still in the very early days of the Web, but I'd been running the Lou Reed site for a few months.

After a while, I reached out to the band and offered them a deal: if they'd pay for my hosting, I would keep doing their site as a labor of love. And thus rocknroll.net and poihq.com were born. The hosting itself is another set of stories.

Along the way I joined Poi's email fan list, the Poi Pounders (a *poi pounder* is a stone used to grind taro leaves into a food called *poi*, which is common in Hawaii, where Frank is from) and later called Place of Refuge. On that list I met a bunch of people who are to this day very dear friends.

Poi's bassist at the time was a tech-savvy guy named Brent Olds, aka Astro. He helped me gather info from the band and even came to my dorm room to help me work on the site. How crazy is that? A rocknroller hanging out at Willard!

And through Brent, I met Chaka who managed the group and later Ken who helped us do cool Web stuff, and eventually everyone who has floated through the Poi universe over the decades.

The web site I built helped foster the community growing around the band. We streamed rare music clips and videos before there was SoundCloud or YouTube to make that easy. We sold out a show with online ordering, before that was a thing. We had members of the band blogging and taking pictures from the road

MEETING MY HEROES

(I gave them disposable cameras and then scanned the pics when they got back). Basically, it was totally ahead of its time.

Me, shooting Poi Dog Pondering for the band's 40th anniversary (and my 30th), 2024

If you look back at CDs from that era, like Liquid White Light, you'll see me thanked in the credits by the nickname the band gave me: webboy. Later I would shoot the covers of the 2-disk *Live at Metro* set.

All the while, I kept shooting. Poi has always let me shoot whatever I want, however I want and from wherever I want. Poi shows were my sandbox and my playpen. And I learned so much shooting them that I took with me for all of my other shoots. I wouldn't be the photographer I am without Poi letting me play.

At their first Ravinia show (and the first band ever to sell out Ravinia — Google that!) the venue didn't really know what to do with rock shows. They assigned me an escort and tried to severely limit where I should shoot from and for how long. Chaka stood up for me. "He's allowed to practice his art with the same freedom we practice ours." After that, I went up in the catwalks.

Part of it was fun to push things, but I also always felt an incredible responsibility to capture every moment and detail in those shows — which is hard when there are 20 people on stage, and visuals and dancers and film loops and lights and the light bulb of death swirling over your head.

But eventually they needed someone who wasn't hand-coding it all in his spare time and moved the site to a different developer. That's a whole different story. As the tools have gotten better and easier, I think Frank does it himself now.

I have kept shooting every show I can and have put together a couple of books and a kickstarter-funded site that archives my poi dog pondering photos.

I have so many memories of this band, its fans, and its music. With my actual family too. Gifting my mom Palm Fabric Orchestra to listen to during treatments. Or Max helping put together the First Day band to march my kids and their mates to school on the first day. Meredith joining me for a show they did at Wrigley Field and Frank playing peekaboo with her from the stage. Or young Me taking the purple to the red to the blue to hang out with the band at their Pilsen space and putting CDs in their cases to mail out with press kits, and then riding the Halsted bus all the way home with Susan. The crazy shows at Shelter. Or Rodman's birthday party. Or the weird fundraiser at the fashion show, me shooting in a tux because it was black tie so why not.

So many real rock moments. And by "real," I mean what it's like to be in a band that doesn't play arenas but gets together and mails their own stuff.

This is a band that's pretty much DIY everything. I don't think I could live the dandy life that Frank lives – sailing the rock seas on tour busses with a guitar, a notebook and a pillow being all he needs – and wine, of course. But I have mad respect for how his life and his art revolve around themselves, and feed each other. The sustenance of art.

I can't say enough about how just nice and genuine literally everyone associated with the band is, and has been for the 30 years I've now known them.

Oh right, the misunderstanding.

After the Kickstarter, the band let me sell some of the books at the merch table. Frank even talked about it on stage and he told the story of that first article. He'd read it at the time and thought that I was just using my press credentials to get closer to the band.

Which was, to an extent, true. He picked that bone with me at the time. I told him I'd been reading a lot of Hunter S. Thompson and experimenting as a writer with Thompson's gonzo journalism, a theory of journalism that the journalist is not detached, but is part of the story and sometimes even necessary to the story. Frank smiled and he totally got it and forgave me.

I was also doing it because I wanted to tell this band's story. I wanted more people to hear them. I wanted everyone to feel what I felt when I heard that band. From that first show, and every one since.

It's been a long time since I interviewed anyone in Poi Dog Pondering. When we chat before or after shows, it's not deep interview stuff. We talk about our kids and their softball games, or current events, or we reminisce. The words from Frank that speak to me are the lyrics themselves: "The only thing that speaks the truth is the eloquence of passing time. The spoken word is a jacket too tight."

But after the Lounge Ax Palm Fabric Orchestra set, when I sat down with Frank and Susan I wrote this:

> Susan described PFO as "Beauty." Not as in the harmonies being "beautiful" which they are. Nor as in the beauty of the ideal where a group cares so much about their art that they are willing to blow off a major label deal to pursue it. Nor as in the beauty of the harp or the violin, or the sly and oh so shy smiles that Poi exchange as they build off one another. Although all are worthy of the word.
>
> No, Susan speaks of the concept of "Beauty." The very idea of the word. She told me "just listen and write what you hear," and I'm sorry, Susan, but I cannot do that. I cannot write well enough to put into words what you all have put so gracefully into the music of Vague Gropings in the Slip Stream.

So in that sense I fail as a writer, which is a hard thing to put into print. I have covered the event but only glanced at the story. Palm Fabric Orchestra must be heard. They can not be written about. If you don't find the album the first place you look, try another, then a third. Don't give up, whatever you do. Then sit in the dark, or in the light, put it on head phones and see what happens. See if a band with a harp, violin, piccolo, and acoustic guitar can move you. Close your eyes and smile–or try not to–and describe what you feel when you fail. See if you do better than I did.

I like looking back at that passage. Because music isn't just music. Music is the thing that holds us all together. Music heals, as they say on KEXP. Music can lead us to a community. You are not alone, as they say on KEXP. Music can bind us to our friends. Music is how we measure the moments. To borrow a phrase, it's the soundtrack of our lives.

For me all of that exists with Poi Dog Pondering and the knowledge that when I'm moving along the photo pit at the front of the Vic, camera in hand, that I am standing exactly where I'm supposed to be.

| *Poi Dog Pondering, 2023*

NICK TREMULIS
ON GIVING BACK AND PAYING FORWARD

Queen's performance at Live Aid is considered by many to be one of the best moments in live rocknroll history. Live Aid was a concert to raise money to combat famine in Ethiopia. It was watched live by something like one in every five people on Earth and raised $100 million. [Note: Ozzy Osbourne just doubled that with his farewell concert which raised $200 million for a series of charities. RIP Ozzy.]

It was all organized by one guy, Bob Geldof, who was in a band called the Boomtown Rats, which had a hit or two in the 80s. In other words, he wasn't really anyone special. But he had an idea, and some chutzpah and got all of these amazing bands to perform for free and got just about everything — from the venue, to the plane tickets to bring the bands to London — donated. Every dollar raised basically went right to the charity.

I've never met Bob Geldof.

But I did meet Nicholas Tremulis. He's a Chicago musician and a mainstay of the scene here. As such, he knows a lot of other Chicago musicians. He and Jon Langford even hosted a radio show on WXRT. I got to hang in the studio one night as Frank Orrall of Poi Dog Pondering joined him and sang a few songs.

Like Geldof, he wanted to help people who needed food. So

he started an annual benefit called The Waltz, after a famous concert film about The Band (with a capital 'B'.)

It was a pretty massive undertaking and I was lucky to get to work with him on it for a couple of year,s via my Metro friends Jenny and Sharyl. And of course it was hosted by Joe Shanahan, Metro's owner, who is a massive supporter of Chicago, the music community and the community at large. Joe's a mensch, too. I built the Web site and then documented the show itself. One year I also shot behind the scenes backstage and at rehearsal the night before at the Lakland Bass factory. Nick was warm, welcoming, friendly, appreciative and a pleasure to work with.

Legends played these shows, like folks from Wilco, Mavis Staples, Ronnie Spector, Billy Corgan from Smashing Pumpkins, Ian Hunter from Mott the Hoople and Hubert Sumlin and David Johansen (more on them later).

They were great evenings, filled with music and camaraderie as well as unusual pairings like Billy Corgan and jazz singer Kurt Elling. The Nicholas Tremulis Orchestra served as the house band, shifting genres and eras with finesse. Hosted at Metro, each show went way into the night and a lot of money was raised to fight hunger. Not $100 million, but a pretty nice check.

At the end of the day, Nick is just a good human. Plain and simple. He was in a position to do some good in the world and he did it.

I include him here because "giving back" is something I should be better about, too. But he did inspire me to not just give back but pay forward, following his example. Perhaps I'll tell that story a little later, too. He also had me shoot portraits (again at Lakland) of a super group he put together with Rick Rizzo (Eleventh Dream Day), John Stirratt (Wilco) and Bun E. Carlos (Cheap Trick) called Candy Golde.

No, he wasn't a star the size of Geldof's Rats. Nor could he pull off Live Aid. But whoever you are, and whatever scale you work at, you can make a difference in your community.

Nick is a stand-up guy for it.

BILLY CORGAN
ON GIVING BACK AND PAYING FORWARD

At first, I wasn't a Smashing Pumpkins fan. I went through a phase in college where I leaned against a lot of music I would later come to appreciate. But eventually *Mellon Collie and the Infinite Sadness* won me over. I covered that tour for *Addicted to Noise* and shot the Pumpkins for the first of what would be many times.

It was an interesting moment for the band. They were closing out what would be their most successful tour for their most successful album. But they had just fired drummer Jimmy Chamberlin after he and a bandmate OD'd (the bandmate fatally) on tour. The band seemed to sense the changes happening and Corgan said during an extended jam near the end of the show, "We are murder, mayhem, malicious malcontents ... misguided and misunderstood. This is the last glimpses and shines of what we started here in Chicago, nine years ago. Everything that follows from here is a different trip." He then had the houselights brought up so that everyone could share in the "special" moment before continuing: "Nine years ago we never dreamed we could play to this many people ... No matter what happens, we shared this time together. It was special. It was great. We send you a message of love, trust, compassion and grace."

I was glad to have been there to witness, as *Mellon Collie* is still one of my favorite albums. But I was much more a witness to the next several chapters.

Eventually I would get to meet Billy and Pumpkins (rehired) drummer Jimmy Chamberlin. Pretty sure I met Billy initially during the Waltz shows at Metro (see Meeting Nick Tremulis). But after the Pumpkins broke up the first time, I tried to shoot Corgan's post-Pumpkins project, Zwan, in St. Louis. Sean and I travelled down for that show, as it was one of the first announced Zwan gigs. They played a little club called the Galaxy, but didn't want press coverage yet, so we just watched and listened. The Galaxy was hard to find in pre-GPS days, as was pretty much anywhere to eat in downtown St. Louis. Sean and I paid a dollar to a guy at a gas station to point us toward a restaurant that was open. Not great.

Billy also played a series of solo shows at the Hideout around this period. I'm told the Hideout's owner wasn't sure he wanted the shows there, but Billy said he had new material he just wanted to work out someplace small and informal. That vibed with the Hideout's ethos, so Tim gave him the green light and his usual enthusiastic greetings.

But anyway, later Zwan would play part of a radio station festival at Tweeter Center (headlined by Kid Rock). This is where I would meet Pam, and also get my first photos printed in *Rolling Stone*. So kind of a big day. Thanks, Billy.

I then shot a multi-night run of Zwan shows for the band at Metro. And later, Billy's first-ever solo acoustic show, again at Metro. I was the only one he allowed to shoot that show, with a set that was decorated like a living room (and maybe with artifacts from his actual living room.) He knew the Metro so well that when there was a hum in the sound system during soundcheck, he made someone go up and turn off the vintage lights in the back of the balcony. The lighting guy was dubious but Billy was right. The hum stopped.

Those pics would wind up in *Rolling Stone*, too. Thanks again, Billy. Although that shoot also taught me an important

MEETING MY HEROES

lesson: make clear the terms of a deal in advance. I didn't do my due diligence of getting things in writing so we had a little disagreement over ownership of said photos. That was my bad.

In short, there was a period where I ran into Billy a lot. Even at shows of other bands, he'd be hanging out backstage. And, somehow, so would I.

Billy at the time had a reputation for being a little difficult in general and I found him challenging to talk to at first. It wasn't really intimidation. It was more that sometimes it's important to go beyond "hey, I'm a fan" and try to get yourself on more equal footing. Equal footing is a better place to have a conversation. It's more relaxed, honestly for both parties in a conversation. Lou Reed was supposedly kind of similar. For Lou, you were supposed to talk about guitar gear or Tai Chi to get comfortable.

With Billy we found middle ground with our love for the Cubs. So that's what we tended to talk about. Once we got into baseball talk we both could relax. And it was cool that Billy for a while knew who I was.

Billy Corgan performs at the Waltz benefit at Metro. This photo appeared in Rolling Stone magazine.

It's important to learn how to talk to people. Even important people. Even awkward people.

Besides loving Billy's music in all its incarnations, I always appreciated that Billy seems to just like living out his boyhood dreams. Maybe he does things to impress and pay back his younger self, too. Like dressing like Rick Nielsen as he joined Cheap Trick onstage and flipping non-stop picks as Rick does. Or when he sat in with Poi Dog at Dennis Rodman's birthday party, singing Bowie's "Heroes." Or all of his fascination with wrestling.

Jimmy was totally different. We sat in Smart Bar, the club beneath Metro. He bought me a beer and chatted like we had known each other for a while. Totally easy-going and able to carry his end of a conversation with ease. Many years and lifetimes later, I'd run into him at the airport in San Francisco. He was an investor in a start-up out there. I approached him while we were waiting, re-introduced myself and we talked tech until boarding time. We talked about my book and I invited him to the book launch party. (Narrator: he didn't come.)

But it's also important not to confuse your heroes with your friends, even if they are friendly. Billy was still hard to work with, and stood me up on a shoot that I thought had been all arranged, but maybe one that no one had told Billy himself about.

It could just be that he existed at a different plane of "rock star" than I was used to working with, even if he was also local and a guy I ran into around town.

Billy is still in the Smashing Pumpkins (with Jimmy again) and they played with Green Day at Wrigley Field. I took my son, which shows how much life has changed since I met Billy back in the day. I was closer to my son's age then, than to my age now. Andrew enjoyed the Pumpkins and sang along to Green Day and it was a fantastic evening.

But it was great to see Billy live out another fantasy and perform at the home of the Cubs. He posted on social about how much it meant to him, and I could see that and feel it and I very much understand it. That alone would give us plenty to talk about backstage, for sure.

| *Zwan, from my first shoot to appear in print in Rolling Stone*

114   BILLY CORGAN

THE CALENDAR PROJECT
ON THE IMPORTANCE OF CONTACTS AND CONTRACTS

At the height of my photography career, I wanted to do something to give back. But also something to push myself. I didn't know a lot about lighting. I'd never worked with an assistant. I'd never really done portraits. But hey, I'd taken *a* class and I knew a lot of people. So, largely inspired by Nick Tremulis and the Waltz I decided to combine all the things. I approached a local charity, Rock For Kids, which helped raise money to provide music education in Chicago public schools. It was pretty tied to Metro and WXRT (both of whom were photo clients of mine) and had an auction I had contributed prints to, so I knew some folks there, too. I reached out and suggested I could photograph Chicago musicians in their favorite locations in the city and then we could do a calendar of the images. They were super enthusiastic and I got the green light. Now I just had to will this into existence.

    I needed 12 artists to agree. I started, of course, with Frank Orrall — and did a really informal, natural-light shot of him in front of the Picasso statue downtown. It was a little awkward because a huge part of portrait photography isn't photography at all, it's working with people (known as "models" in the business). And I wasn't good at that ... yet?

    I needed help. Chicago photographer John Shearer was a

friend of mine and also shot at Metro and helped me cover all the shows at Tweeter, where I was also House Photographer. He graciously accepted my unpaid offer to assist on the photos. I explained he was basically going to be doing the lighting because while I now had lights, I didn't have a ton of experience using them. He wanted to play around more too and thought this would be a fun project.

So I started reaching out to musicians I knew or knew people who knew. Or I went to shows, worked my way backstage and pitched them directly. I don't remember off-hand anyone saying no. Though some had their "people" say no later (cough, Liz Phair).

Through the sheer force of my will, I lined up an incredible slate.

After Frank, John and I teamed up to shoot John Stirratt of Wilco who was also performing in a band at that time with his sister, Laurie. I met John at Farm Aid, where Wilco were performing (and joined on stage by then state Senator Barack Obama!).

They invited us to the home in Logan Square I think they shared at the time and it was super awkward. Frank and I at least knew each other well by that point. Here I was, in the living room of very important strangers, working with John for the first time. And working with posing people for the first time, and basically working with lights the first time. And I'm sure it all showed but they were patient and cool and we all made it through. In the end my favorite shots were some of the less posed ones when we handed them guitars and they played and we all found ourselves more in our comfort zones. We also took some portraits of their dog.

We shot Rick Nielsen of Cheap Trick at Piece, a pizzeria/brewery he was an investor in (pro tip: the pizza is sooooo good). My original vision was to shoot him in the brewing part back by the kegs. But once we tried shooting that it just wasn't really working out. So we quickly shifted gears and did something even more off-the-cuff and natural. The final shot was so much more authentic. Few people are better at promoting themselves in a light-hearted and fun way than Rockford's own Rick Nielsen. And that's exactly what we wound up with.

Then we sat down and had a beer and chatted a bit. Turns out he was a big Mac geek. He basically started sharing his favorite memes with me and I learned that he had the best and most appropriate email address ever, which, no, I won't share, even though I can't imagine it's still current.

We shot Scott Lucas of Local H in the studio he was recording in. Also a chill and fun shoot. Robbie Fulks at the Lula Cafe in Logan Square. Archer Prewitt from the Cocktails and the Sea and Cake had us shoot him in the Garfield Park Conservatory, so I got to learn the ins and outs of getting permits from the Chicago Park District. (I also learned that getting approval to shoot at the Bean required permission from the artist, Anish Kapoor, and that it would of course then need to be referred to by its actual name, *Cloud Gate*.) Jon Langford, a Chicago treasure himself, wanted to be photographed at the Field Museum. All the appropriate levels of whimsy were involved in that.

Sallie Timms, Kelly Hogan and Nora O'Conner

Archer Prewitt

Scott Lucas of Local H

Cheap Trick's Rick Nielsen

Robbie Fulks

Jon Langford

Frank Orrall

John and Laurie Stirratt

Nicholas Tremulis

Knowing that Sallie Timms, Kelly Hogan and Nora O'Conner had all worked at Hideout, as well as performing there with all of their various bands and collaborators, that seemed the natural place to photograph them – not on stage, but behind the bar. By that time, I was getting some experience and confidence and was able to work better with John (having a vision of the lighting) and with the musicians (having a vision of the poses) and things were going along well.

Nicholas Tremulis also wanted to be photographed in his home, which he even set-designed for us by hanging postcards with his most recent album cover all over his piano (or maybe they were always there?). Despite being mostly known as a guitarist, his piano was his happy place. One of his kids poked their head in so we did some shots of the two of them as well.

It wasn't all perfect. I worked with Billy Corgan's manager to set up his shoot at the Adler Planetarium where he was doing a record release party for his first solo album. John couldn't make it so I called Columbia College and asked if they had any students who might be able to help. That's how I met Dre. She came, wandered the museum with me and we scouted out a great location that had both cosmic and musical significance: Stonehenge! Dre was great and we came up with some creative lighting, did a bunch of tests, compensated for what Billy was wearing (black) and the height differential between Dre and Billy (not insignificant) and got all set up. We had plenty of time to kill, it turned out.

Periodically, I wandered up stairs where Billy was meeting with fans and... no one had told Billy that this shoot was happening. He was tired and had been traveling and meeting and greeting. I implored him that it was for a good cause and he literally just had to come down and stand on a piece of tape we'd marked the location with and let me burn off a couple frames. Five minutes and we could get it done.

He wasn't feeling it, which I get but which was also kind of disappointing.

But nothing would compare to the eventual disappointment of the charity pulling the plug.

Not Billy Corgan, sadly. Photo by Andrea Coan

We had most of the months shot. We had lines on the remaining people. We were starting to plan for year two (bands not solo musicians). We had a printer lined up to do a series of large-scale prints to get signed for the auction. We had a printer lined up for the calendar and were looking at paper samples. And the charity's director didn't have sign-off for the upfront costs from the board, who thought it was too big of an expense to get printed.

And just like that, it was done.

I tried one other organization and had a couple of promising meetings with them, but no dice. These days we would have just Kickstarted it and been done, but at the time there wasn't anything I could do.

Exhausted and disappointed, I shelved it. These images still haven't been widely seen, which is a shame.

Point is, even for charity projects, get stuff in writing. Set clear goals and expectations up front. I had dotted all my I's and crossed all my T's on my end, getting release forms and permission from locations. But I also assumed that the other end had its due diligence done. And well, assumptions....

So I accomplished some of my goals. I learned a ton and met a lot of great people. I got more confident and broadened my shooting experience.

But I failed at the real reason, the whole "give back" part. Who knew that would wind up being the hardest. Non-profits are strapped for cash (hence the need for fundraisers) and often staffed with hard-working volunteers and limited paid staff. I'd inadvertently created a burden for them, I guess, instead of just handing them a pile of money. Sadly, I couldn't self-finance the printing costs.

That said, if anyone has any ideas how to turn this around 20 years later, I'm happy to help.

THE DEAD MILKMEN
ON FANDOM AND THE ENABLEMENT THEREOF

When I think about the movie ~~Almost Matt~~ *Almost Famous* I often think about the role of the young journalist's mom in his career and story arc. She dropped him off at concerts and picked him up afterward. And she let him go off on tour into the world generally referred to as a three-headed Cerberus where "rocknroll" is the most virtuous.

At one point in the movie his mom winds up on the phone with one of the band members her 15-year-old is touring with and tells him, "This is not some apron-wearing mother you're speaking with – I know all about your Valhalla of decadence and I shouldn't have let him go. He's not ready for your world of compromised values and diminished brain cells that you throw away like confetti. Am I speaking to you clearly?"

Now, my mom would not have cared for the Dead Milkmen had she listened. She wouldn't have liked some of the words they said in their songs, nor that her son was listening to them. She was, and is, pretty strict about many things.

The Dead Milkmen, Live at Chicago's Metro.

Which made it all the more amazing that she pulled me out of school one time to take me to a record-signing at Repeat the Beat in Dearborn. They were doing this in-store event before a show she knew I was disappointed to be too young to go to. (She would not, for the record, have driven me there and dropped me off, but it's plausible my dad would have gone with me, as he did for Billy Joel. And yeah, I wasn't going to be allowed on tour with them!)

I didn't miss school much, as a kid. And I don't miss work much now, as an adult. But Ferris Bueller had it right. Life moves pretty fast, and if you don't stop to look around once in a while, you might miss it. These days I celebrate that with Day of the Dad. Sometimes I wind up with days off that the rest of my family doesn't have. Often it's Veterans Day, which is right near my birthday. I spend the day doing projects around the house, or grabbing a matinee that no one else wants to see. Then and now, there's a lot to be said for playing hooky.

Obviously I have my parents to thank for helping me meet many childhood heroes. We met Mr. Wizard, the "Supermarket Scientist," who had a book and did TV appearances doing chemistry experiments with household goods. I got to meet Shuttle astronaut Brewster Shaw (I had his business card, too, and signed no less, but left it in my breast pocket and it went through the wash. This was far from the only thing I would do that with. Why do I still use breast pockets?). They would take me to baseball card shows, where I met folks like Tigers Catcher Matt Nokes. They did let me go to a concert by myself, now that I think about it, but I drove myself. That was how I met Lou Reed the first time, hanging out by the stage door.

I knew of the Dead Milkmen because when I was in middle school I would stay up past my bedtime listening to the high school station nearby, WBFH. I could only listen until 10pm because it signed off the air entirely at that hour because, well, the DJs all needed to go to bed. So did I.

WBFH is also where I first heard Mojo Nixon. WBFH played a lot of the Dead Milkmen. I immediately fell in love with the crazy, quirky lyrics of songs like "Punk Rock Girl" and "Bitchin' Camaro". I bought all their records (and tapes). Even my favorite Detroit Tiger, Jim Walewander, loved them. They visited him in the clubhouse before a Tigers game when they were in Detroit. That day, he hit the only home run of his major league career. A reporter asked, "Did the Dead Milkmen give you inspiration?" Walewander replied, "No, they gave me a T-shirt."

The summer after high school, I did get to see the Dead Milkmen live at a memorable show in Pontiac where they had put an amphitheater on top of a parking deck. (It hosted some amazing shows, looking back, Porno for Pyros with the Flaming Lips! The Beastie Boys!). During "Bitchin' Camaro", there was a lot of talk about (Chevy) Camaros and their Pontiac rival, the IROC. The security guys got into it with one of the bouncers pointing to the other dramatically indicating that he owned an IROC. Hilarity ensued. I hung around long enough to meet them again.

By college my fandom was pretty set and became well-known and really one of the first times I would say that musical preferences became at all intertwined with my identity. Friends would have me recite the song "Stuart" on the way to classes. It was a song about burrow owls, the pitfalls of being a daredevil, and, of course, it's about what the queers are doing to our soil.

And then years passed. The Dead Milkmen kind of came and went and came back again. But I got to shoot them at Metro in 2009, and tweeted back and forth with the band and with singer Rodney Anonymous and met Dave Blood's sister, who was also shooting the Metro show. My teenage self was very psyched, and my adult self was pretty geeked, too.

Now, I've got my kids listening to all these bands, and singing "Stuart" too. So much in the world has changed, including their listening on Bluetooth headphones tied to their Apple Watch instead of corded headphones and boomboxes. But they're still probably listening past their bedtimes. And conspiracy theories about the queers are raging more now than ever. It's a good thing the music is a constant.

JIMMY G. (NOT JOHN CUSACK)
ON POWER, LACK THEREOF, KINDNESS AND UTILITY

One unfortunate way my photos often get used is when the people in them die. I have a fair number of clips of famed director (and Ghost Buster!) Harold Ramis.

He directed a film called *Ice Harvest* which starred John Cusack and his sisters Joan and Ann, and Connie Nielsen. All of them appeared at the opening, which was held in Chicago. I was hired by Getty to shoot it. I shot photos of Ramis (whom I guess didn't get photographed too much in later life). One made it onto the front page of the print edition of the *Chicago Sun-Times*. I also got pics of the Cusack siblings together, which based on my clips, was somewhat rare. Apologies to Joan, because it gets used pretty often and it's really not the most flattering shot of her.

Oh, and Nielsen was dating Lars Ulrich from Metallica, so I got some photos of him, too. It was an interesting night.

John Cusack also starred in many other great movies. One was "*Say Anything,*" which is why he interviewed Cameron Crowe (see the preface). He was also in "*Eight men Out,*" and "*Gross Pointe Blank,*" both excellent films. But my favorite of his movies is one of the all-time great music movies, *High Fidelity*, which has the added distinction of being set in Chicago and full of other Chicago people, locations and references. It's based on a book by Nick Hornsby. That's set in North London, where Hornsby was from. But when the script was adapted by John Cusack and his writing partners, the location moved to Cusack's home town.

There was a lot of excitement in 1999 when it was filming around Wicker Park and other neighborhoods. Scenes were shot at Double Door and Lounge Ax, and the film is littered with Easter eggs from Chicago's turn-of-the-century alternative scene.

For the film's 20th anniversary, we got tickets to go see it on a big screen with Cusack doing a post-show Q&A as part of a tour he was doing (with a couple different films including *Say Anything*, but of course Chicago got *High Fidelity*.)

We went downtown, parked, got dinner and headed to the theater, only to find a notice taped to the door that it was canceled. Turns out it had been postponed far in advance, but there was no notice on any of the relevant social media, nor did they bother to email or call me, despite having all of my contact info.

What pressing other engagement did Cusack have?

Well, he spent the night rage-Tweeting that his posts were being throttled because of his views on Palestine.

I'm going to be petty and hold a grudge so John Cusack isn't the hero here. But after the Cameron Crowe night, my attitude toward him warmed back up I'm glad to be back appreciating him for his quintessential Chicagoness.

But here comes the segue.

Cusack's character in *"High Fidelity"* manages a record store. In one of the scenes he tells one of his coworkers, "I will now sell five copies of The Three E.P.'s by The Beta Band." He proceeds to spin the track "Dry the Rain." I suspect that scene sold way more than five copies. I know I bought one and was an instant fan.

Which led me to interview them a couple years later in 2002 at the Vic Theater.

I was pleased to learn that their guitar tech was none other than Jimmy G (Galocy), who will be the subject of this chapter.

Jimmy G was part of the Poi family around the time I met all of them. He was a guitar tech among his other hats, and just one of the nicest guys going, in a troupe of nice people. I don't think I've ever heard anyone speak ill of him. Poi tested his skills in any number of ways. Can he catch a guitar thrown off-stage between songs? Yup. Can he sing back-up when the road manager, Eric "Honkeytonk" Buehlman, sang lead on Elvis songs or "Sweet Caroline"? You betcha. And can he keep up with the mad array of instruments played by the 17 or so folks on stage? He sure could.

The folks in the wings of Poi shows over the years – including, off the top of my head, Spike, Ian, Martin, Luke, Marco, AJ, Ryan (now out front keeping time), Mark, Chaka, Tina, Ronnie, Jimmy, Frankie, Kim and of course Lemondrop Matt – really are part of the family. Some have been there forever. Some left us too soon. One became a member of the band. One had a song written about him. Even Poi's humble photographer has been name-checked on stage a couple of times over the years.

| Jimmy G (Galocy)

Jimmy was, I think, the first loss in the family. I didn't know him that well. I won't pretend I did. But his loss was and still is felt in the community in and around this band – in the Poi family and of course his family, whom I've had the privilege to get to know a bit over the years as well.

To bring this back to the story, I did a pre-show interview

with the Beta Band for MusicToday.com. Before the show got started, the power went out. The band tried to persevere, at points with the emergency lights, playing acoustic. At one point Jimmy was holding a flashlight on them and also helping keep things in check when the band was passing out champagne from the stage to pass the time. I wrote the unexpected newsy part up for Bill board.com.

Jimmy seemed at home on stage, side stage, back stage.

That was the last time I saw him. He was gone just a couple months later.

I know I try to keep these stories coming back to the lessons I've learned from these people and the ways in which they were a hero. I was maybe too young when I met him to put it all together. But in retrospect...

"Be kind" is too easy a lesson and one I could attribute to many people in this series. That said, kindness is important, of course, and a bit of a lost art in America these days. Many "role-models" are anything but.

But more importantly as it applies to Jimmy... be useful. Do your job, and then some. Take whatever skills you have and use them all the ways you can for whomever you can find to use them for. Then learn new skills you can use in more ways for more people. Volunteer.

I've been thinking about this recently as it relates to my softball coaching. I've come to think of myself as the "utility" coach. I'm by no means the best coach, or the most skilled or the coach who can tell at a glance when you're dropping your hands on your swing. My super power is showing up (underrated as a super power, btw). Once there, I do whatever needs doing, whenever. Keep score? Shag? Hit flies? Set up warm-up areas for the pitchers? Coach first base? Shuttle kids to the games? Sure. Happy to help.

Being kind and being useful is what gets your name on top of a post like this instead of a bunch bigger names dropped in this somewhat meandering chapter.

DICKY BARRETT AND STEVEN PAGE
ON FINDING THE STORY IN UNEXPECTED PLACES

As I've said, sometimes the story isn't where you think it is. Sometimes, like with Sterling Morrison and Moe Tucker, you have to go find it. Sometimes, it finds you.

My college roommate, Jon, grew up outside Boston. He was a fan of a ska band called the Mighty Mighty Bosstones, and he played them for me a lot until I just started playing them for myself. He, Jack (who would later be a roommate in my first post-college apartment) and I started 3 of the first 2,500 or so sites on the Web. Jon's was about the Bosstones. Mine was about Lou Reed and the Velvet Underground. I think Jack's was a little more eclectic, but had a lot of Lovecraft involved.

Anyway, there was a summer music festival called H.O.R.D.E. and in 1998 or so it came through with the Bosstones and the Barenaked Ladies on the bill.

There was a media area set up in a gazebo off to the side of the stage and members of the press like me would wait there between acts, maybe have a bottle of water, maybe work on our notes. From time to time band managers would come out and set up interviews with their artists, which was kind of unusual — normally it would take a lot of work to set those up.

A bunch of us were hanging around when up strolled Dicky Barrett, the lead singer of the Bosstones. I'd interviewed him a couple years earlier for *art + performance* at Northwestern, inspired by Jon, I'm sure.

A young woman there had asked his manager for an interview and he went straight for her. "Hey, are you from *Spin Magazine*," he asked. "Yes!," she replied, "do you want to talk now?" And he said, much to her surprise, "No, I don't. I hate *Spin*." And he started to walk away. "Wait, I'm from *Spin* online," she called after him. He paused almost as if considering and half-turned back. "Nah," he said. And off he went.

| Dicky Barrett

She was sad because she thought she'd lost her story. I suggested she look at it another way: He came out and told you off in person, to your face. He didn't send his manager back. He wanted to do it himself. Now *that's* a story. And see, it was, wasn't it? (I don't remember if she agreed.)

I love Dicky for that. And also for the overall no-nonsense way he seems to live his life. And not in the way some people say they "just speak the truth" as a cover for basically being rude. But I digress.

This was one of those moments that illustrated that sometimes, maybe even often, the story isn't the story you thought it would be. Sometimes the story sneaks up on you. Sometimes you tell the story. And sometimes the story tells you off.

Bonus lesson: Later that afternoon, the manager of the Barenaked Ladies came and grabbed me. He asked if I wanted to interview Steven Page, one of the band's singers. I wasn't prepared at all but they were a fun band so I figured, "why not." As we were walking back to their tour bus the manager told me that they had a new album out and a couple of other useful tidbits.

Then I sat down with the leader of this super-quirky Canadian band and asked a couple basic questions and just let the conversation go. I couldn't possibly be anything but relaxed because, despite not being prepared, there also wasn't anything at all at stake. My editors weren't expecting this interview either.

We had a great, relaxed conversation. If you've ever listened to one of their songs, you can imagine that Steven Page was a clever, funny guy — and he was. We talked, I took notes and then we were done.

Sometimes, the best stories tell themselves. If you listen, and ask just enough questions to keep the conversation going.

THIRD EYE BLIND
ON FINDING THE STORY IN UNEXPECTED PLACES, PART II

Third Eye Blind have somehow endured. They had some hits in the mid-to-late '90s that have stuck around even today. But they were poppy and mainstream and clearly I should be mocked as a sell-out for liking the infectious hooks of "Semi-Charmed Life." But yeah, that's a great track.

Part of the reason they hold a special place in my heart is because of the time I met them. I was doing a story for a site called JamTV that would later be bought by *Rolling Stone*. It was a big deal and a sound crew was going to record audio for a precursor to a podcast. I was going to write an article.

The publicist had sent me a press kit, which in those days meant she mailed me a copy of the CD, a glossy photo and a folder with a bio of the band and some copies of articles other people had written about them to give me some background. They were just beginning to break so there weren't really a lot of articles and so far there was almost nothing on the Internet.

So I did what prep I could, arrived early at Metro, where they were playing, and hung out for not just their soundcheck, but the opening band's as well.

Finally it came time for the interview, I sat down with the band, the tape rolled and we started talking.

It was one of the worst interviews I've ever been a part of. To start off, we did a round of introductions and when three members of the band had introduced themselves, I said to the final member, "you must be," whatever the drummer's name was.

But no, they'd fired the guy listed in the press kit and this was someone totally different.

Awkward.

It went downhill from there, largely because the singer came off as an egotistical jerk and clearly enjoyed talking to people like they were idiots.

Afterward, my editor said he physically cringed as he listened to the tape.

But he was also amazed at the story I pulled out of the experience.

My lesson here is to never give up on the story. It's in there somewhere, even if it's not where you originally thought it was. I don't mean this is the same way as with the Dicky Barrett story in the chapter before this. I mean in the way that sometimes you just have to keep looking until you find it — often in the shadows, or around the corner, or in the characters on the periphery as with this story.

If someone's a jerk, keep asking the questions you need to ask, don't let them get in the way of doing your job.

And if you like a song, it doesn't matter what anyone else says — just play it louder.

Here's a quick excerpt from the article I wrote:

"A tall platinum blond named Patrice is passing out the second round of steaks backstage at Chicago's Metro before 3eb's sold-out show. She had to run out and buy round two because the opening band, Reef, mistakenly chowed the first batch of steaks. Patrice says she's from the Mayor's office. Apparently, superpol Richard Daley's daughter is a big 3eb fan and asked her dad to pop for dinner for the band. The tab? $300."

And here's the part I left out of the article, which is ... another way to meet your heroes.

After the show, I saw the woman who bought the band dinner (on her own dime, clearly not the Mayor's.) She was heading out for a drink with the singer. I caught up to her and asked her if the huge expense was worth it. "Oh, yes," she told me, and off they went.

WESLEY WILLIS
ON KNOWING THE WORTH OF YOUR WORK

Wesley Willis was a punk rocker in Chicago and also an artist. The *LA Times* summed up what most people knew about him, describing him upon his death in 2003 at age 40, "Wesley Willis, a 6-foot-4, 320-pound former homeless man who channeled his schizophrenia into an unlikely career as a rock music cult hero."

I had friends who knew him a little bit. Or at least interacted with him frequently. One worked at the Wicker Park Kinko's, where Willis would copy fliers or covers for his tapes. She said he had "demons" but was a gentle guy despite his size. But it was also intimidating that his preferred method of greeting was head-butting people.

I liked his music, at least in some contexts.

As a fine artist he generally drew with markers on poster board. He'd show up at shows at places like Metro and sell them. That's where I met him. He was sitting on the steps with a pile of his artwork. I flipped through and found one I liked. It was a split panel of Wrigley Field and the river, looking along by the Sears Tower. Which is not named Willis Tower now after Wesley, though it should be.

How much, I asked. Fifteen, he answered. How about $10, I

countered. He countered with "How about $20." "Ok," I replied, clearly out-negotiated, and handed him a twenty.

But he also had a point. I think we all too often devalue our own work. And then people try to further devalue it or get "a good deal" on it.

We also don't always have obvious norms and values around *our* value. I thought I was in a situation where one might haggle. I was kind of wrong. Sometimes when people are hiring you, they might work for a huge corporation, but that doesn't mean they have more money budgeted for that role to offer you. Sometimes they do. I had a boss who offered me slightly *more* than I asked for and bought a ton of loyalty and respect. Regardless, it's important to know your own value, or what tradeoffs you're willing to make.

I try to make money from people who have it, but also to be aware of where the margins are a little thinner. I was at Metro that night to shoot a show as House Photographer. This was not a role I was paid for. Whatever amount I would have asked for would have been a deal breaker. I realize I was the only one in the building not getting paid directly for being there, and maybe that makes me a sucker. But I was willing to work for free in exchange for: access, ease of that access (I'd send an email to Jenny with the shows I wanted to shoot and she'd hook me up. No need to track down and pitch publicists), and keeping the rights so I could license the images elsewhere. I met great people, including some heroes of mine, made new connections and got extraordinary life experiences to boot. Working for Tweeter Center as their House Photographer I got all of that and also got paid, because they were an enormous corporation and could give me a small stipend which basically covered gas and some other expenses. It worked well for everyone involved, I hope.

I'm not quite sure what that Wesley Willis piece is worth today, but his artwork hangs in galleries. And in Andrew's room.

Wesley Willis, you knew how to drive a hard bargain and I have much respect for that. Rock over London. Rock on, Chicago.

HUBERT SUMLIN AND DAVID JOHANSEN
ON THE CONTRAST OF LEGENDS

Hubert Sumlin was one of those people who never quite made the big time, household-name fame, but inspired a lot of people who did (and countless others who didn't either). He was a blues guitarist. Played with the greats most notably as Howlin' Wolf's sideman, but also with Muddy Waters. He inspired Eric Clapton and Keith Richards of The Rolling Stones. "Hubert was an incisive yet delicate blues player," Mick Jagger said in a statement when Sumlin died. "He had a really distinctive and original tone and was a wonderful foil for Howlin' Wolf's growling vocal style." (Keith and Mick paid his funeral expenses.)

I met Sumlin a couple times. He played two benefits I worked on. One was the Waltz with Nick Tremulis. He was performing with David Johansen, himself a legend as the frontman for punk stalwarts the New York Dolls, who later also had some solo hits under the name Buster Poindexter. Johansen was a big blues fan and that influenced his own music. But how these two hooked up I don't really remember. What I do remember is how good they sounded together, and clearly appreciated each other as musicians and people.

Nick Tremulis and a Mt. Rushmore of Blues: Hubert Sumlin, Pinetop Perkins and Honeyboy Edwards

I was helping out on another charity gig called Hopefest (my friend Sharyl who helped put on the Waltz was producing this show, too). Pinetop Perkins and Honeyboy Edwards were performing, too. That's quite a lineup. I mean, Honeyboy Edwards played with Robert Johnson in the '30s!!! All three have passed now. Pinetop was considered the last of the Delta Blues musicians when he died in 2011. Studs Terkel did a reading too. How cool is that? And I got to meet Sumlin at his hotel and drive him to the venue in my little Saturn. He was sweet, and polite, and funny and charming and I was honored to chauffeur him around a bit.

I had a bunch of duties that day but one of them was to shoot a story for my friend Brian J. Bowe who was then the editor of a revived *Creem Magazine*. Each issue featured a portrait of a musician or band holding a prop *Creem* beer can with its mascot, Boy Howdy, on the can. Johansen had done one of the first such shoots 30 years earlier with the Dolls. So Brian interviewed them both and I took some photos of that and then sat them down to do the portrait. My assistant John Shearer and I had gotten to the venue super early to set up the lighting for it and get the shot staged just right. And then, as photographers often have to do, sat around and waited hours to get the time with the artists.

MEETING MY HEROES

David was handed the can and became rather surly. "What? No one told me this was a beer commercial?!?" he growled. Brian tried to explain the set-up and history. David still bristled. I got three frames off before he got up and walked away.

David Johansen and Hubert Sumlin for Creem

But John and I had put in the work, spent the time and were ready. Three frames was enough. Nailed the shot, which did indeed run in *Creem* (that, too, was an honor for me). I think it captures everything rather perfectly, including the joy and humor Hubert brought to every situation and the way he just slapped his leg and laughed at David's reaction to everything. Seems he was a good foil for David Jo, too.

And yes, all of this wonderful, contagious love for everything is ironic for a man famous for playing the blues.

I was glad to meet him and eavesdrop on some of his conversations and watch him with his legendary peers and watch them all just appreciate each other. And the magic. And the music.

So take whatever road you can to meet the storytellers. Arrive early, stay late, and be ready when they are. Pick 'em up at their hotel. Because stars are often late, rarely on time and worst of all, sometimes they're early.

I mean, really, what better do you have to do than wait for your man?

| *Johansen* really was a sweetheart, as captured here.

SHANNON HOON
ON STOPPING THINGS BEFORE THEY START

My friend and former colleague, Anne, has a newsletter featuring her writing and thoughts on creativity called Glisk* In a recent issue, she wrote about... me, and my newsletter. She wrote about how music can bend time. To me, that means how hearing music can put you in a time, or a place. My daughter Meredith talks with clarity about the first time she heard various songs. Where she was, what she was doing. All of this makes me think of... Blind Melon. All these years later I still remember this feeling. And the noise and the sweat.

One of the best shows I ever saw, and there are those who roll their eyes at this, was Blind Melon playing at Northwestern. My roommate freshman year was Jon R. (Side note, I have never lived with someone who wasn't named Jo(h)n or Pam.) Jon had gotten their CD for Christmas and we played it on repeat when he got back. So we were excited when they came to campus. We were right up front. The stage was less than a foot tall, and the ceilings were low so the band was right on top of us, rocking and sweating away in the tiny space.

It was still in heavy rotation in my room the next year, with a different Jon, Jon M. We would play it loud on Friday afternoons as we cleaned the room in advance of hosting parties under the disco ball of room 121.

Years later, I was again excited to see them at Metro. I had a phone interview before the show but didn't get a chance to actually meet Shannon Hoon. His wife had just had a baby and he was full of hope for the future.

Yet just weeks later, he died of a drug overdose in New Orleans while on that tour.

There are a million lessons here but all I can say is that it's far far easier not to start something than it is to stop it. Shannon knew that and fought it, but in the end, it got to him. John Popper, the singer from Blues Traveler, talked about his own struggles, and his band's, with addiction. His issues were with food and weight. But one member of his band also had issues with drugs. "He went to New Orleans. That's like if I went to live in a Burger King. It's not going to end well." New Orleans is many kinds of city, but largely a city of temptation.

Sadly, the interview I did with Shannon ran in some papers after he had died, so I wrote a follow-up obituary we could distribute quickly.

I still listen to Blind Melon when I'm cleaning the house.

TIM HARRINGTON
ON HOW MY DOPPELGÄNGER UNDERSTOOD THE ASSIGNMENT

Somewhere around 2010 I learned I had a doppelgänger. Over the years I'd been told I looked like various celebs mostly depending on how much hair I had and how long it was. When I was a teenager it was Paul McCartney. When I was older, Frank from Poi Dog thought I looked like John Cleese. But nah. My real doppelgänger is Tim Harrington, the singer of Les Savy Fav, which has been described as an "art-punk band."

| *This is not me. This is Tim.*

I look at photos of him and think, yup that's me with a beard.

Others have said we could be brothers. One described the resemblance as, "Unnerving."

In 2013 after my book launch, I posted a photo of him on Facebook and just played it off like it was me thanking everyone for their support. Some friends were tipped off by the Heineken Light he was drinking that it wasn't. Others who had seen me at all recently realized I couldn't possibly have grown a substantial beard that quickly. But some lifelong friends who hadn't seen me lately didn't bat an eye.

At the time I learned this I'd mostly stopped shooting and wasn't even going to many shows. I thought it would be fun to meet him and take a selfie, but it was also unlikely. The band also stopped releasing new material and seemed to play big festivals when they came around. I kind of gave up thinking about it.

Then I was at an end-of-season party for softball and my friend Matt said he was going to a show later that week at the Empty Bottle. I had oddly just been to that little club for the first time in like 20 years to see Bug Club, a KEXP fave. But Matt said he was going to Les Savy Fav! And the game was afoot.

Still, the show was on the birthday of one of my kids, and during an otherwise busy week, and even if I went, I didn't have any hook-ups to get me backstage. Also it was super sold-out. So I kind of let it drift. But then Matt texted on Thursday that he could get me a ticket. The kids, even the birthday kid, told me I had to. Pam gave me one of those "do it, or shut up about it" looks. And I decided to head out for a late show on a school night.

I understood the assignment. I had to get a selfie with this guy. It was binary. Anything else was failure. I assumed it would be easier to make this happen before their set, during the inevitable downtime pre-show. Honestly, I also assumed I would want to go to bed after the show.

As you've seen, there are many ways to meet your heroes, just in terms of the functional mechanisms. I tried them all on this night:

- I tried hanging out by the door to where I thought the dressing rooms were. But first, there are a couple of those at the Bottle and second, none of them had a bouncer. So there wasn't anyone I could just ask and plead my story to.
- I tried the guy at the merch table, but he was with one of the opening bands and didn't seem to know anyone else.
- I tried the guy at the front door and asked if there was a tour manager around. But sometimes clubs and/or bands are so small they lack infrastructure. Door guy was like, I don't even know if they have one. No one seemed overly willing to take up my cause.
- Matt offered up a Hail Mary in that he knew the owner of the Bottle(!). But that seemed like overkill.

Then, as we're watching the opening band, and I look up and there I am.

I mean it was one thing to see photos and think, "I really look like that dude, if I had a beard." It's another thing to actually see him face to (my) face. He was rocking out. Just hanging out against a wall, jumping up and down and really appreciating the opening act. Matt and his friends clocked him about the same point I did and I quickly moved closer to him.

Fanboy/stalker mode activated (sometimes the most successful method is the most straightforward.)

Empty Bottle has kind of a weird layout for a venue in that the stage is in a corner and the room is sort of L-shaped. So I had to make sure I had sight lines to his several possible exits, because I assumed he couldn't stay for too long, he had his own set to prep for. After a couple of songs, Tim started moving and I just ambulance-chased so closely that Matt's friends thought I'd already talked to him and he'd agreed and we were just walking off together to make it work.

There was a small clearing before he got to the door and, as I did with Martha Stewart, I tapped him on the shoulder and he turned to face me and it was right there. My face. I explained that he was my doppelgänger and asked if we could move somewhere with light and take a selfie. I'm not sure he fully engaged, nor that he thought he was looking at himself too. It's maybe easier for me to think, that's what I'd look like with a beard than for him to remember what his pre-beard face looked like. But he humored me and he found a light behind the window curtain which would suffice. He also immediately understood the assignment. He used his hand to cover his beard, I did the same, we took one selfie and he was gone.

And then it was done and I could enjoy the rest of the night. Matt seemed to know everyone in the crowd, all of whom seemed to be Oak Park parents. The owner, Bruce, showed up and we chatted with him for a bit.

I texted the photo to Pam, who said, "Omg. Good thing I know your wedding ring." And she clearly showed it to the kids. One of whom guessed wrong. But texted, YOUR EYE COLOR LOOKS BROWN AND IT WAS MAKING ME SECOND GUESS MYSELF."

In fairness, I had a bit of a hard time with it too. I posted on Facebook and many people guessed wrong, but most figured out which one I was.

The show itself was amazing and I was thankful I didn't have to spend it wondering how I was going to meet him.

Watching Tim perform was just weird. He'd have an expression or make a face, and it would be my face. It was also a gift. I don't have to wonder how I'd look with a beard. There it is. I don't have to wonder what I would look like if I had tremendous self-confidence or at least zero inhibitions. There I am: Shirtless. Dancing. Throwing myself around. The clear center of attention at all times. He's a world-class spit-taker.

Tim spends a fair amount of the show wandering through the crowd with a very long mic cord. At a couple of points he even walked out of the Bottle and was singing on the sidewalk and talking to passersby (or people who stepped out for a smoke.)

It's kind of amazing that my doppelgänger is also in many ways therefore Bizarro Me.

I mean, my doppelgänger could have been an insurance guy, or a coder. Maybe we would have passed each other on a sidewalk or sat near each other on the el. But no, he's a singer in a band, and I'm a guy who photographs bands.

He seemingly has no cares, and I wear a shirt when I'm swimming, though largely because I'm pasty. He "dances like no one is watching" but also knows that everyone is watching.

He also fronts a great band and played a heck of a set. 10/10, recommend.

After the show he was still wandering through the dispersing crowd. Matt said he saw them play a church once, and afterward the band shook everyone's hand by the door as they left, like a priest at mass.

This was a little less structured, but no less sincere. He took more selfies with people who looked nothing like him, and were not as well lit. He hugged folks. He got some water from the blue cooler in the back, not the orange one next to it which he said (during the show when he also helped himself while still performing) "The orange one reminds me of Home Depot and they're all MAGA now."

I went over to thank him again for the selfie and tell him that one of my kids didn't recognize me. He again was nice, but also seemed far off.

"Crazy kids," he said., "Crazy kids."

This is me. And Tim. But not necessarily in that order.

MEETING MY HEROES

NICK KELLY
ON CREATIVITY AND THE JOYS OF FANDOM

Thirty years ago we got a demo tape of *Johnson* by the Fat Lady Sings at the *art & performance* office. Several copies actually. And I think most of the editors picked it out of the pile and thought "OK. It's an Irish band with a song called Drunkard Logic. Intrigued."

Several of us took it back to our dorms and apartments and popped the cassette in and gave it a listen. Turns out it was a really great album. It lived in my Walkman during the brutally cold winter of '94.

Sadly it was the band's last. They didn't break through in the U.S. and called it a day.

Never got to see them live, but my friend Sean I always joked that if they got back together we would have to get on a plane.

When I went to Ireland and Scotland a few years later I would pop into record stores and ask after them. The indie rock clerks were always a little taken aback and begrudgingly impressed that this random American came in and asked after a local Irish group that I had basically no business having ever even heard about, let alone really liking. But there wasn't much news.

Still, I kept an eye out. Nick Kelly, the band's singer and songwriter got a job in advertising and started also making short films.

Ten or so years ago Nick came to Chicago to bring his film to the Chicago Irish Film Festival. I was excited to go see it and even more excited that he would play some songs after the debut. I emailed him about a photo pass and he assured me that wasn't really necessary.

Sean, Izenstark and I trekked down to Beverly. The film was great and his 'concert' was basically just him and a guitar in the cafeteria at the Arts Center. If I recall correctly the sound system wasn't really working so he eventually just sat down in a chair on the floor with 20 or so of us sitting around him in a circle and played. I finally got to hear one of my all-time favorite songs performed live and the acoustic version was lovely but not quite the same as the full-band. Regardless, it was great to meet him.

Time passed. We all got older. Nick kept making music here and there. And films here and there. And commercials for his day job. During the pandemic he, like many artists, played some shows from his living room and porch and streamed them on Facebook. His kid would wander through looking for Legos. All of it was sweet and Nick seemed very genuinely touched that people from around the world were tuning it, tipping a few bucks and enjoying the old songs. He also seemed to enjoy dusting them off. He struck me as someone who had had a moment, realized that moment was gone and moved on with his life. Always scratched his creative itches. But also as someone who was finding the nostalgia a little endearing.

Then an amazing thing happened. Nick essentially called our bluff. He announced a reunion show with the Fat Lady Sings celebrating the 30th anniversary of *Johnson*. In Dublin. Essentially on my 50th birthday. Pam said I should get Sean to go with me and that if I didn't go I was never allowed to call myself a fan again. So we found flights on discount Icelandic airlines and I found myself in Ireland for my 50th.

Sean, Nick and 50-year-old me

I again emailed Nick and asked for a photo pass, which he again said wouldn't be a problem. I also found a small fan community on fb and posted my excitement about coming and asked the locals for hotel recommendations. Nick himself gave a detailed and thoughtful reply with some great options and we promptly booked one within walking distance of the venue.

Being alone on my 50th itself was kind of weird. I got in before Sean did so I went to an Irish steakhouse and sat myself at the bar. I told the bartender it was my birthday and I'm generally a bourbon drinker but wanted to try some Irish whiskey. He made me an incredible smoked cocktail. After I was done with my steak, they brought out a 50th birthday dessert for me, which was quite kind. He pulled over a waitress and they sang "Happy Birthday" but when they got to the part with my name they realized they had no idea what my name was. The waitress quickly covered with "Mr. President," with all the Monroe-esque suggestion. Well played.

Sean and I had both been to Dublin recently with our families so we did some more adult touristy things like the IrishRock 'n' Roll Museum and a literary pub crawl.

Then it was showtime. We grabbed some dinner nearby after trying and mostly failing to make friends with the bartender at the venue. Thankfully, we had bought our tickets well in advance, because the show sold out. It was fantastic. Two sets, one from each of their records. Nick said it was the longest show they had ever played. I got to hear all my favorites with the full band, who hadn't played together in so long that the guitarist had to buy a new guitar for the show. Oh. And I got a birthday shout out from the stage. Can't top that.

There was an aftershow gathering upstairs that Sean and I got invited to join. In typical small-world style, we wound up chatting with a couple from Chicago who were Poi fans with mutual friends.

But of course the highlight was getting to thank Nick for everything. We chatted for a while and the part that stood out was when he started talking about creativity. He described creativity as "long bits of messing around and then sudden bursts of brilliance." This was specifically in relation to a weird guitar tuning only he uses. Certainly it applies more broadly, too.

I admire the way Nick has never stopped creating, even if it's not for the huge audiences the Fat Lady Sings had likely hoped for when they came over to "do America" in the '90s. I also admire the fans who don't care that this wasn't the biggest band in the world, it was still a big band for each of them.

Nick's latest band, Dogs, recently debuted their new album. But I wasn't able to hop over for that.

Perhaps ironically, the Dogs album, *Joy*, contains a song called "All my heroes are assholes." Sounds like Nick needs better heroes.

MAX WEINBERG
ON THE ROCK & ROLL HALL OF FAME

A while ago, I watched *Back to the Future* with my kids. In one scene, Michael J. Fox's character plays "Johnny B. Goode" and wows the crowd with a song and a sound that was still a few years off. The band leader calls his cousin, Chuck Berry, to tell him about this new sound he heard. That's funny because "Johnny B. Goode," was a song written by Chuck Berry – one of many that would help define a new genre called rocknroll.

In 1995 the Rock & Roll Hall of Fame and museum opened in Cleveland, Ohio, over Labor Day weekend. I was still in college, but school hadn't started yet. I had a friend who lived there and it wasn't that long a road trip, so I got myself an assignment to cover it, which meant I also got a free ticket to the opening concert. Lou Reed fronting Soul Asylum and dedicating "Sweet Jane" to his recently departed bandmate, Sterling Morrison was one highlight in a night filled with legends doing their thing. Google the lineup sometime (or seems you can watch the whole thing), but it included Aretha Franklin, James Brown, Little Richard, the Kinks, Johnny Cash, and the Boss, whom my kids were taught early to know is Bruce Springsteen (they know "the Man in Black," too.) His band, the E-Street Band, backed a good many of the performers, including Mr. Chuck Berry.

That afternoon there was a press conference and the E-Street drummer, Max Weinberg, was one of the people being interviewed. He was asked what it's like to rehearse with Chuck Berry, who could be demanding and who was also known not to even show up for rehearsals.

Max looked at the reporter and said, "If you have to rehearse 'Johnny B. Goode,' you shouldn't be playing it.. When Chuck Berry's foot goes down you play. When it comes up, you stop. And you'd better know the rest."

That's the kind of song it was. Legends grew up on it and was in their, and therefore rock's very own, DNA.

When I told this story to my eldest, I asked "Why is that? How do you get so good at something?"

Mac of course knew the answer: "Practice."

Now, knowing the answer and living the answer are two different things, right kids? But knowing the answer is a good step in the right direction. Beyond that, you just have to do the work. Find the thing that you love as much as Max Weinberg loves the drums. Then doing the work won't seem so much like work. It'll seem like rocknroll.

Funny side-note: At the end of a very long day I wandered back to my car in the lot. The parking attendant saw me and said, rough day for your team. I was confused for a moment. Then I remembered. It was colder than I'd thought it would be and I hadn't packed well. The friend I was staying with lent me her boyfriend's sweatshirt. His Notre Dame sweatshirt. I asked the attendant, incredulous. "Are you saying Notre Dame LOST?" He replied in the affirmative. Which meant that Notre Dame had lost to... Northwestern. And thus started the conversion of my school into a football school, and our Run for the Roses started out in high gear.

KISS
ON MARKETING AND LIMITS

"Once upon a time there was a band that gave its all on stage and shook the stage with bombs and dazzled an audience," Paul Stanley, the star-painted lead singer and guitarist of Kiss told me in a piece I wrote for Live Nation that appeared in the *Sun-Times*. It was a phone interview, but I later got to meet him, too.

Like Joey Ramone, the dudes from KISS believe fully and full-throatedly that KISS is the best band in the history of the world. One thing I wrestle with is the difference between a Bowie, or a Lou Reed or Poi Dog and a band like KISS. The former are always reinventing. The latter, not so much. In all cases, that's by design. I have to say that I tend to like the creative reinvention approach. But I have a certain respect for KISS' take on things, too. Paul Stanley told me, "KISS remains KISS. The last thing we want to be is new KISS. New Coke didn't go over too well. We stick with what's tried and true and what we believe in. What we wanted to do is polish it up and put some new features on the car."

I respect that attitude, as mentioned. Other things, I respect less...

KISS is absolutely a great band and a fun one and one that leans into the entertaining spectacle of it all. It's possible that if you haven't seen them, you've missed your chance. Or at least to see the humans of the band. Supposedly they'll be back as holograms or avatars or some tech-enabled representation of what used to be some of the best, loudest, explosive and raucous shows around. I saw them a couple of times at what was then the Tweeter Center, where I was House Photographer. As such, I was asked to shoot a meet-and-greet for VIPs (fans who had paid extra for the chance to get their picture taken with their heroes). Some of the venue staff also hopped in for pictures, and I asked if Paul and Gene Simmons would sign some photos I had taken of them at a previous performance. Gene is the bassist and arguably the brains and long-tongued face of the brand and machine that is KISS, the corporation. He's also a hit with the ladies.

In the spirit of the Albert Maysels line I've used before, the job of the photographer is to see what everyone else sees but notice more. I like to watch the interactions of the band and especially what's going on away from the spotlight. Sometimes, like with Poi Dog, I catch the sly glances, the non-verbal communications and try to capture all the things that maybe others miss.

With KISS, the moment I remember was a bit less subtle.

Mid-show, I saw Gene seemed to be scanning the crowd. Then I realized he had a guy helping him look for "lucky" people to give after-show passes to!

Gene would point to (almost all blond) women in the audience, or the guy would shine a flashlight at someone and Gene would nod or shake his head. At one point Gene pointed and the guy shone his flashlight and Gene seemed to approve of the choice.

But the guy shook his head. Gene looked at him like, "What? What's the problem, dude." The guy pantomimed a wedding ring. Again, Gene looked at him like, "What? What's the problem, dude."

It's rough getting older. And having times change around you. Not that that was ever right, but even 20 years ago it was way wrong.

MEETING MY HEROES

But that little vignette aside, I always appreciated their music, but more importantly their work ethic and their ability to market themselves and find all kinds of ways to entertain and connect with fans, from action figures to comic books and now to digital avatars. There will always be room for KISS on stage and off, although maybe not-so-much with the backstage anymore.

Paul Stanley of KISS

JIMMY BUFFETT

ON KNOWING WHAT TO ASK, AND MAKING THE ASK

I appreciate people who do what they do, do it well, give the people what they want, and seemingly live the life they want in the meantime. Jimmy Buffett was one of those people. Dude famously only played shows on Tuesday, Thursday and Saturday, to the point that he titled one of his live records that. As he wrote in the liner notes, "When our ship comes in, the party begins. If angst is your diet and serious thought is your idea of recreation, then PLEASE DON'T BUY THIS RECORD. But, if you like the beach, need some escapism and like to laugh, stomp and dance, then you have come to the right spot. And, YOU ARE NOT ALONE."

There's that phrase again: You are not alone.

Music brings people together. Those people can form communities. Loosely, or tightly. For a couple hours or a couple of decades. Buffett's fans were the Parrotheads. There were a lot of them. He reliably sold out the large venues where Pam worked, and where I was House Photographer, and probably did OK on the concessions gross for the day, too. He was a VIP in the concert business, a profit juggernaut on the scale of better-known artists like The Rolling Stones or U2.

I...was not a Parrothead. But I'm glad I had the chance to see the carnival in action in the same way I'm glad I saw the Grateful

Dead, especially when Jerry Garcia was still around. Or Insane Clown Posse. Or Gwar.

And sure, Jimmy Buffett wrote a lot of good songs. He played an interesting role in promoting the Chicago Old Town scene. But really at the end of the day he made a lot of people happy. For the Parrotheads, a Buffett show was an annual bacchanalian festival of liver-function sacrifices, ceremonial (shark-fin) head-dresses, revelry and offerings of cash to their *patrón*, Saint Jimmy. His shows were like prom night, or maybe more like a furrycon.

I didn't actually meet him. I got pretty close. But there are a couple stories I want to share that I think fit into this framework.

One of the reasons I was hired as House Photographer at Tweeter Center (currently the Credit Union 1 Amphitheater) was to decorate the backstage area and catering dining room. For years it was just bare cinderblock. But what if, they thought, we put photos of the bands who've played here on the walls. This was not a novel idea.

One of the catering walls at Tweeter Center, decorated with my photos

I started shooting and printing and framing and quickly decorated the joint. It was a cool gig and I should note it's one Pam hooked me up with, partially because it was the only way we would see each other during summer. She had to be there for pretty much every show, which was pretty much every weekend and then some. By becoming House Photographer, I would be there too and we could run into each other from time to time and maybe even grab a quick bite in catering.

It was also a ton of work and driving and running around (I wish I'd had a step counter in those days).

Buffet played Tweeter toward the end of that first summer. I'd hung a bunch of prints as the summer progressed and that made the backstage look presentable. He was playing Thursday and Saturday and I shot the Thursday show, then Liz Phair at Metro the next night and headed up to Radiohead at Alpine Valley (where I was also House Photographer) the following night.

While we were at Radiohead, Pam got a panicked call from the house manager at Tweeter. Buffet's people were mad that his photo wasn't on the wall. What was the hold-up?!?

It was explained that the photo project had just begun that season and that I'd just shot him for the first time on Thursday and hadn't gotten to print it yet. But when someone is a VIP they get VIP treatment and Buffett was no exception. There wasn't any way to get something on the wall before the show that night. As a compromise, they printed a "reserved for Jimmy Buffett" sign, framed it and hung it on the wall as a placeholder. Everyone was grudgingly happy. Jimmy could ask for things, and didn't really have to care how big of an ask it was.

All of that earned me some brownie points with his management, so over the next couple of years I was invited to get exclusive shots of him and some special guests who joined him on stage – like Martina McBride and Jack Johnson.

Then Buffett was announced as the inaugural concert at Wrigley Field. This was a big deal that they were going to start hosting non-Cubs events there and Buffett was the perfect opener. It also turned out to be a poignant show, as it took place days after Hurricane Katrina hit Buffett's New Orleans.

At the time I was doing a project for Pam's work: documenting the size of the crowds during an especially big couple of weeks with sold-out shows for Farm Aid, U2, The Rolling Stones, and this opening night at Wrigley.

That meant I had the run of Wrigley Field for the day to try and capture the feel of being there for this unique show. I showed up early and walked every corner of the stadium looking for the right angles and vistas. It occurred to me that one shot worth exploring was from behind the stage overlooking the crowd, but elevated so you could get a good enough view. It was hours until the show but I was already in full scout mode.

"Hey," I asked one of the staff, "I'd like to go up in the scoreboard and check that out."

Guy looked at me and shrugged. Sure, I guess. There were likely some radio conversations as people conferred. And then, like it was no big deal, he walked a group of us over to the scoreboard and let us climb on up.

Into. The. Wrigley. Field. Scoreboard.

Pam and a couple of her colleagues also needed to scout this clearly, too.

The scoreboard was fun and I appreciated the privilege of being able to go there. However, it turned out the stage blocked most of the crowd, so it wouldn't be the shot I needed. Still. I got to go in the scoreboard. And walk the warning track. And touch the ivy. And and and.

And shoot the Buffett show. And grab a candid of him with polarizing Cubs super-fan Ronnie Woo Woo. [Of course there is video of this.]

And I also did my job, which is important to note. I really did think there might be a cool shot from up in the scoreboard. Sometimes the shots you hope for don't work out, which is why you make sure you have lots of other options going in, and stay open to things that happen organically (like the Ronnie Woo Woo hug).

It's also important to not be afraid to ask for things. Know what things are big asks and what things aren't. And by that I mean what are big asks for the people you're asking them of. It was no big deal for the guy at Wrigley to pull the ladder down and let us in the scoreboard. It just happened to be a really really big deal for me.

Finally, whether you're a Deadhead, or a juggalo, or a parrothead, or a Swifty, or a poi pounder or whatever... find your people, and find the reasons and occasions to gather with them and celebrate.

LIN BREHMER
ON BEST FRIENDS, AND POWERING THROUGH THE MORNING

Lin Brehmer was the morning DJ on WXRT for most of my Chicago-living life. Like John on KEXP, he had a couple of mantras. One, that he was your best friend in the whole wide world. And two, that it's great to be alive. And it was great when he was alive.

Lin Brehmer was a Chicago treasure. When he died in 2023, it seemed every social feed in Chicago was filled with photos of one's friends standing next to him. Because as he always said, he was everywhere. He was smiling in all the photos, and it was genuine.

Lin Brehmer, always the host but also one of the crowd

I don't think I have a photo with Lin because when I was with him, I was the guy with the camera. I was kind of the House Photographer for XRT for years, back in the day.

I by no means knew him well but I enjoyed the times I spent with or near him. Having an early drink on Opening Day with him and Jon Langford (who might have been one or two ahead of me). Or seeing him at shows. Or events I was working.

He seemed to live every day and eat meals to the fullest. He got me through many a morning, seeming to take on the exhaustion and hangover of an entire city - playing the music to power us through. Because the thing with waking up to Lin Brehmer every day was that he always sounded like he had a longer night, and rougher morning than I had. And yet, there he was. At work, doing his thing and entertaining his best friends in the whole wide world.

So what excuse did I have for dragging?

His Lins' Bin audio essays were so amazingly literate, both in terms of music and the spoken word, that it's hard to describe. And it's sad that licensing means almost none of them are available anymore, although this might have been his final one. He had just returned from cancer treatment and wanted to thank everyone for their support. I remember listening to it in the car on the way back from a softball bullpen and explaining to Jane who Lin was and why it was significant.

One of the last things he posted on his socials was this interview with Frank Orrall of Poi Dog Pondering – just two old friends hanging out in a backstage bathroom, telling stories.

After *Livability* named the awesome and thoughtful Winona Dimeo-Ediger my successor as editor there, they flew her up to Oak Park to get a brain dump from me, and also see one of the Best Places to Live in action. We planned to go to a Cubs game, but it was raining so we hung out at the Gman waiting it out. I told a couple stories about Lin, who was also one of the biggest Cubs fans the team has ever known. Lin had a Cubs fan level of hope, but he applied it to...everything.

MEETING MY HEROES

Eventually the game was rained out but we burned our tickets to duck in so I could at least show her around Wrigley. As we emerged, we of course ran into Lin waiting for his wife to pick him up outside. He really was everywhere. I told him that I'd just been telling Winona what an institution he was for this great city of ours.

Even though it had been years, he clearly remembered me and asked about Pam, who had known him better and longer. I mean, this guy must have known thousands of people in this town and been known by hundreds of thousands. But he kept us straight in his head. He was always friendly and approachable and in good spirits. And always kind.

I don't know how he did it. Any of it.

Looking back, that would be the last time I'd see him. I'm glad to have one more chance to say some nice things to him, too.

And although he'd glare at me for name-checking what he considered the worst song ever written, he truly built this city on rocknroll…

DAVID BOWIE
ON GRACE, AND BEING A HERO JUST FOR ONE DAY, BUT ALSO EVERY DAY

When I think about the term *hero*, it often is soundtracked by David Bowie. He is one of my top five favorite artists and "Heroes" is one of my top three favorite Bowie songs. DJ John Richards has been known to play 30-minute sets of that song with different versions and covers.

Bowie was so creative, so inventive, so willing to change course – yet his career followed a discernible path.

Nothing was random; it was a constant evolution.

When my kids were young, they seemed to think that every song was written by David Bowie. Which is my fault. I played a lot of his songs for them as part of my ongoing efforts to teach them the ins and outs of rocknroll.

David Bowie was both the broccoli and the dessert in their music education. I can't say how proud I was when nearly five-year-old Jane demanded his just-released *Blackstar* for her shower accompaniment. "It's my new favorite," she said.

I was lucky to see Bowie in big rooms: *Sound + Vision* tour at the Palace of Auburn Hills; Area One at Tweeter Center; with Nine Inch Nails also at Tweeter. I also was treated to shows at much smaller ones: The Vic; Detroit's State Theater (solo and with Tin Machine); The Aragon; The Rosemont Theater; and even at the Borgata casino for what would turn out to be one of his final U.S. shows. The Polyphonic Spree opened that one.

David Bowie and Nine Inch Nails

In '97 Bowie Chicago tour stop was at the Aragon Ballroom. It's a terrible place to see/shoot a show so I decided to go home to Detroit and cover his show at the State Theater instead. I brought my sister, so that was fun, and made a new friend in photographer Jennifer Jeffrey.

However the night before the Detroit show Bowie was the mystery performer at the Vic Theatre for a a Miller-sponsored show called a "Blind Date." Blind Dates were a series of shows where folks would win tickets to see a band, but they wouldn't know who the band was until they showed up.

I was already scheduled to cover the Blind Date, which turned out to be an amazing show (of course) with the Chemical Brothers opening. (The following year I would meet/see Garbage and the Red Hot Chili Peppers on the Blind Date bill at Aragon.)

Now I wound up covering two shows early in the tour. Bowie liked the pieces I wrote (!) so I was invited to meet him at his Aragon show which I then attended after all. I don't normally get all fan-boy-geeked out, but I was anxious to meet him. The PR person was introducing the other people at the meet and greet and they were all radio station head honchos and label muckety-mucks. Bowie was polite. The PR person got to me and had no idea who I was. "I'm sorry, who are you?"

I introduced myself.

Bowie actually perked up and said "oh, *you're* Matt Carmichael, it's great to finally meet you" and told me how he'd really liked the stories etc. I was thinking, "You've got this backwards, I'm a 23-year-old schmo and you're Ziggy Stardust," but it was totally disarming and we had a nice chat about Chicago jazz, how the Aragon was reportedly where Glenn Miller debuted "In the Mood," and Bowie reminisced about his early tours in the U.S.

I had him sign two of the pics from earlier in the tour. I gave one to my sister as a thanks for going new wave in the '80s instead of hair metal and introducing me to so much good music. The other photo hangs by my desk. I guess he thought the pic was somewhat Inferno-esque. He inscribed it, "Another bad day for Dante."

Bowie could have been a lot of things: He could have had a massive ego, he could have been a jerk. He could have signed some things and wandered off. But that's not what happened. And there's the lesson. If you know that everyone who meets you is likely to be intimidated (because they're fans and you've probably changed their lives somehow) or bored (because they work for a label and meet everyone), the best way to deal with that is figure out who is who, be polite to the bored ones, but disarm the intimidated ones with charm, grace and humility.

It turned a fun story into a completely unforgettable experience. He was a hero year-round, but an extra special hero for me on that one day.

MEETING MY HEROES

"Another bad day for Dante" – David Bowie

WILCO
ON COMING HOME

This tale isn't about meeting Wilco...yet. Although it stars Wilco and this story had to happen in order for that meeting to happen. This is a story of transition, and home.

It's early 2000. Twenty five years ago, today. I mentioned in the Steve Yahn/*AdAge* story that my job was moving to New York. What I didn't mention was that they wanted me to move with it. New York is a great place and I really loved visiting the city – on someone else's dime. The handwriting was on the wall, so when I would go to NYC (almost monthly in this period), I'd always be thinking in the back of my head about whether I wanted to live there.

The answer was typically no, I didn't. It was just more of everything... more expensive, more crowded, more dirty. Chicago also doesn't lack for things to do. If you're bored here, that's on you. This is where I was making a life and home for myself.

Another factor was my photography. On the side, I was a young rock photographer and had achieved some success and was somewhat known in the community. In Chicago I was one of a handful of people shooting shows on a regular basis. The fact that Chicago had a scene so full of opportunity – so many bands, so many shows, so many special, unique experiences – and yet so few took advantage...Well, that played to my advantage.

One such venue was Lounge Ax, which was sadly closing because some idiot moved in next to a rock club and then got upset that it was noisy. He kept filing complaints with the city and somehow this one selfish jerk was able to shutter a beloved part of the Chicago scene.

Don't be like that guy.

In its final week, Wilco played a poorly-kept-secret show, billed as "Summer Teeth." Jeff Tweedy, Wilco's leader, was married to one of the clubs' owners, Sue Miller. I didn't have an assignment confirmed and wasn't on a guest list, but I walked up to the front of the line with camera bag slung over my shoulder. It was January and people had been sitting outside the venue for hours and hours in the cold. Some had driven from other states. Doors weren't open yet but I walked confidently up to the door. I nodded in recognition to Dan, the longtime door guy, who recognized me, too. He waved me in and I was set. Fellow photographer Marty Perez greeted me at the bar and we chatted until doors opened, at which point we moved to the stage and took our usual places.

The show itself was one of those quintessentially Chicago shows: a little sloppy; a little fun; somewhat serious; imbued with deeper meanings; and a gathering of old friends, family and new acquaintances coming together to enjoy the music that binds us all.

I knew I could never pull this off in NYC, where I'd be one of too many rather than one of a small group of concert photographers. As Sinatra sang in his famous Chicago song, "My Kind of Town," "Now, this could only happen to a guy like me, and only happen in a town like this." I didn't want to give that up. I stayed in Chicago and kept shooting shows.

Tweedy, in Wilco's lyrics, has sung about many things that are important in this tale: storytelling, dreams, and home. Searching for a home. Coming home.

> "If you're selling yourself on a vision
> A dream of who you are
> An idea of how it should be
> And a wish upon a star"

Home isn't just a place, physically. Home is where you feel comfortable. Home is where your people are. Home is the place you can't wait to escape. Home is the place you come back to.

For me, home is the house in Bloomfield Twp, where I spent the first 19 or so years of my life, and it's the beach down the road from there, past Weird Bug Rock. Home is also Cranbrook, whose campus and buildings I know inside and out. It's Northwestern, but really by that I mean Willard Residential College where I lived for my years on campus. It's Wrigley Field and before that Tiger Stadium. It's the cottage in Holland, which is the only home I can't really go back to. And of course home now is Oak Park.

And home was pressed up against a low, dark, noisy stage – camera strap wrapped once around my wrist, bag cinched around my waist. Listening to my hometown band, in my hometown club, doing a thing I loved in the only place I could possibly do it.

Walking into that show really was one of those tipping points in my life and most of the stories you've read so far flowed from that. I'd shortly land the House Photographer gig at Metro and my photography career would really start taking off. I'd settle down for real in Chicago.

During this period in the early part of the century I was working for a company that did consulting work for airports. It wasn't the most demanding gig, so I was able to keep shooting, up to 80 shows a year. It was a lot.

Then I got a call from *Crain's Chicago Business*, a sibling publication to *AdAge*. It was 2005 now. They offered me a ticket back into journalism full-time, which sounded amazing. That's how I became the Research Director, aka the "Lists Guy." After I started working there, my editor told me he considered my photography a potential conflict of interest and all of a sudden, rocknroll.net stopped.

Which isn't to say that I stopped meeting my heroes. I just developed some new heroes in some new phases. Crain was kind of a home. There I worked on a project called "MarketFacts" which was page after page of data and infographics and maps. That project led to my switch back to *AdAge*, which led to my interest in demographics, which led to my book, which led to my job at *Livability*, all of which led to Ipsos. I developed new heroes along the way, and you'll meet them in the next section of stories.

But I want to come back to this idea of home. At *Livability*, it was central to the work I did there, helping people find their best place to live. That thinking and research is part of what brought me to Oak Park.

It centered on one question: Will where I live allow me to lead the life I want?

| Wilco performing one last time at Lounge Ax

PART FIVE
PROFESSORS, PEERS AND PROFESSIONALS
WITH EACH NEW JOB, I'VE GAINED NEW HEROES

ELISSA SLOTKIN
ON POWER, AND GETTING THINGS DONE, AND HAVING A PLAN

Elissa Slotkin is one of my few political heroes. As a member of the U.S. House of Representatives she won in some very swingy districts in Michigan. No she is Michigan's United States Senator, having won as a Democrat against a well-funded opponent in a state that Trump carried. Before running for election, she worked in the CIA and Department of Defense, serving several tours in Iraq. She's lived a life of public service, called to it after 9/11.

Her family also did a great but very different service to our nation: inventing the Ball Park Frank.

Slotkin has helped see the country through tricky times (she was the person who delivered the Presidential Daily Briefing to President Obama). And her districts have had challenges, too. She became the first member of Congress to represent not one, but two school shootings: Michigan State and Oxford High School, where she gave the graduation speech for that class. Not an easy assignment.

Through it all, Slotkin has managed to stay above the fray.

Concentrating on issues of national security and job creation, she's about as moderate as they come, and has proven herself to be quite pragmatic and effective at keeping her job by keeping the people of Michigan happy and being able to speak effectively to very different groups of constituents.

And she was at Cranbrook when I was, graduating two years behind me. Which means there will still be a Cranbrook Senator, as 2025 also marked the end of Senator Mitt Romney's term. He was in school with my mom, and she opened for him at an alumni event as she won the "volunteered a lot and made a direct difference in the school" award the year he won the "dude's a governor and might run for president" award.

I'm not sure what it says that I don't have a lot of political heroes, nor whether that says more about me or about politicians. Nor have I met or interviewed many political folks. Other than mayors of mid-sized towns, whom I talked to and met often during my *Livability* days. Mayors are a good general blanket set of heroes. For the most part, they can't mess around getting caught up in whatever political nonsense happens at the state and federal levels. They have to functionally run their city. The parts of government that impact everyone, every day: plowing streets, taking out the trash, schools, parks, permits, zoning, etc.

Mayors get stuff done. Slotkin does, too.

As a kid I got to go to the Capitol with my family on a spring break trip to D.C. We got to meet our representative, William Broomfield, who served in Congress beginning in 1957 until 1993. We saw his office, and I got his business card and autograph and later he sent me a signed photo of then-President Ronald Reagan. All of that was pretty cool for an elementary schooler.

Closer to home, two of my kids had the chance to "Page for a Day" for Illinois Senator Don Harmon, whom we found to be gracious and generous. They enjoyed meeting so many of the Illinois leaders and touring Springfield. (Andrew got pandemic-ed out of the chance, sadly.)

Later, my friend Sean hired me to help decorate the office of his boss, Congressman Mike Quigley (IL-5), who had just been elected to his first term and needed photos of his new district to hang on the walls. Later Sean would hook up my kids with a Capitol tour and a chance to meet Congressman Quigley. Much had changed in the Capitol, as we had one of the first tours after the pandemic and the attempted insurrection of January 6th. It was a much more fortified Capitol, but Rep. Quigley's staff were excited to have visiting citizens back, and he met with us and answered questions and showed us his office, which still includes some of those photos.

Congressman Mike Quigley (IL-5) in his office in front of a photo I took for him

MEETING MY HEROES

But back to Senator Slotkin...

In late 2023, I was working on an issue of *What the Future* about the future of Conflict. She was my first ask and we were able to make the interview work. She got it done, even if that meant she called a staffer on the phone, and her staffer held the phone up to her laptop as we did the interview over Zoom. The staffer seemed to be doing laundry in the background. It worked. It got done, and that was the point.

The interview was quick and focused and she closed it by saying, "The polarization in the U.S. is the Number One threat to our national security because it completely freezes decision-making." And, she added, our enemies are watching.

We have to figure out a way to get back on track as a country and focus more on all of the things we agree on and less on the things we don't. Any discussion of polarization that doesn't talk about how outside forces are swamping Americans and our allies with disinformation and propaganda is missing a big part of it. Our enemies and other actors have profited greatly from stoking the fires and fissures among us.

Slotkin will try to be a part of that solution, I'm sure.

I got to meet her at a fundraiser event at the home of Christy Hefner, who lives in one of the most storied condo towers in Chicago. It's where many of the names in *Crain's Who's Who* (which I used to edit) have lived. And many of those old familiar names were in the room as she spoke. She was just as measured and smart and impressive and genuine and pragmatic in person, in a small closed-door event as her public persona. I won't go into specifics because these things are generally considered off the record.

But I will say broadly that Slotkin talked about how conservatives have been playing a long game: impacting policy, electing officials at all levels and especially working the courts and the SCOTUS to their advantage. "Where is our 10-year plan," she asked the room.

I didn't have a good enough plan when I actually met her.

Hopefully you'll note that's unusual in Meeting my Heroes. I usually have something I want to ask them, or talk about. In some ways I had already made the big ask: The interview had already published. But I did work my way over before she slipped out to make sure I could say hi, and put my face to my name and, yeah, grab a selfie with the future Senator.

Had I more time I suppose I should have seized the chance to lobby for things that matter to me, some obvious and some more pet causes. But it's also good to recognize when you're less important than the other folks in the room, be gracious and not take up important people's time.

Everyone left the event, went back to work and helped her get elected by raising money, or making calls, or knocking on doors. And they all got it done. Now it's up to her, but I'm confident she'll make for a great Senator for the big purple state that is Michigan.

RYDER CARROLL
ON HABITS AND ROUTINES...

I think a lot about how to stay organized and keep on top of tasks. It's not easy, but it's so important. It's something I failed to learn. It's been a struggle, therefore, my entire life. And therefore something I've tried, and struggled, to instill in my kids.

Starting in 6th grade or so, every year during back-to-school time we'd make sure to pick up a small, red leatherish planner called an assignment book. The best ones were from an Evanston bookstore called Chandlers (RIP). It would have space for every day of the school year for me to write down what homework I had to do.

Every year I'd fill it diligently for about a week. And then less diligently. And then really sparsely. By October it would just be blank pages taking up space in my already crowded backpack.

Since then I've spent my life trying (sometimes, in fits and spurts, but mostly not bothering) to find an organizational system that worked for me.

I had hoped with computers and later with Palm Pilots and smart phones that I could figure something out. But no.

I found some good calendar software at the end of 1998 (originally the Palm Pilot desktop software). I've been able to keep that up and can tell you with some certainty where I was on every day since.

But the to-do and other aspects of organization eluded me. I'd kind of given up.

And then my friend Scott Smith posted something on his Facebook page about journaling. I'd read little bits about this world and culture from time to time. As I said, I was always on the lookout. But as I read his post and the responses to it, I started to follow him down a rabbit hole. I read a lot of reviews and blog posts. I watched a bunch of YouTube videos and then I pulled the trigger and bought a notebook, the official Bullet Journal from Leuchtturm.

The Bullet Journal is a physical notebook, which is important. Neuroscience tells how much more we learn with the physical act of writing. (Also, it's an excuse to buy pens.)

It starts with blank dot grid pages, so you have to design your own system and draw it in. You figure out what matters most, and how best to keep track of it. That was hugely useful to me. I'd always wanted a notebook where I could keep longer term ideas, as well as a to-do list. I also wanted something where I could easily blend work stuff and life stuff. The Bullet Journal led me to a way of doing that.

October 1, 2018 was a Monday so I started my journal at the start of a week and the start of the month. I have kept it up nearly every day since. It has helped me immeasurably. I use it to record things I need to do, thoughts about projects I'm working on, and other things from time to time like softball stats, the House points we used to award our kids and even topics for the Meeting my Heroes newsletter..

The Bullet Journal was created by a guy named Ryder Carroll and, although it had been around a while, he published a book about it not long after I started using it. The timing was perfect. He did a book signing at the library in Lincoln Square where I wrote a good chunk of *Buyographics*, and thus I got to meet him. I love libraries.

Ryder was chill and approachable in a well-attended talk and Q&A. Among other things, he's got this amazing ASMR voice.

I'm not sure if you could put together an easy demographic profile of those who came out to hear him. But there is one camp that creates elaborate (drawn/painted/watercolored/washi taped) layouts each month and then posts them for Insta-likes. Which seems to go against the rather minimalist approach to the whole idea. Ryder addressed this elephant in the room and said that yeah, there are folks who kind of miss the point. But that he's also heard from people for whom this is the time they set aside to be creative. That's important, too. And if this is their outlet, that's perfectly in line with Bullet Journals.

Ryder talked about how it's a system and a practice. The system is what you put in your journal, and how. Ryder has ADHD and started the Bullet Journal as a way to manage that and all the related noise in his head. One lesson from Ryder, therefore, is that if you have a problem, you're likely not alone. So if you solve something for yourself, you're probably solving it for enough people that you can scale it into a bigger thing and therefore help lots of people.

It's the practice that's really important, and the part I'm still not as good at. The idea is to build the journal into your daily routine.

In the morning you use it to plot out your day and what tasks you want to accomplish. In the evening you spend a couple of minutes reflecting on what you got done and moving forward tasks that you didn't quite get done. You can also use it to write reflections on the day, your thoughts and ideas.

The challenging part is that when things in life are most chaotic, it's hardest to keep it up. Yet, that's exactly when you need the most structure and routine to keep you sane.

I always thought routine and structure were lame and stifled creativity. But I was 100% wrong. Habits and routines allow you to do some critical things without thinking about them. That frees up your thinking time for more important and creative things. This discipline also helps you stay on top of things you need to get done so you don't have to spend so much mental energy keeping track and stressing about what is and isn't done yet.

The Bullet Journal takes all that load off of your head.

Much has been written about habits and routines (try Charles Duhigg's *The Power of Habit* for starters) and I wish I'd understood it all sooner in life.

It's never too late to learn, and never too soon to start trying.

LYDIA CLARKE AND CHARLTON HESTON
ON THE POWER OF
WORDS AND IMAGES
AND OPPORTUNITIES

Oddly I don't have a ton of photographer heroes, and of those whom I admire and respect, I've only really met one: I'm convinced that legendary concert photographer Mick Rock took my photo as I took his at Lollapalooza.

I knew all the Chicago photographers back in the day. From newspapermen like John Sall who dabbled in concerts, or Paul Natkin and Barry Brecheisen who were the only two to fully make a living off of that work in a city of millions. I learned so much from Steve Serio and Erik Unger at *Crain's*.

I once saw Albert Maysles do a Q&A after a screening of the famed documentary film of the Rolling Stones tragic concert at Altamont, *Gimme Shelter*, which he produced with his brother. Maysles said something that stuck with me to the point that I used it as my email signature for a while. The job of a photographer or photo journalist, he said, is to "see what everyone else sees, but notice more." Notice more. That's not as easy as it sounds.

One of my other favorite photographer lines, however, is even more pertinent to me personally. This is that story.

I was assigned to live in Willard Residential College at Northwestern. I requested and applied for that after doing a prospective weekend there. I stayed with a guy named Ed Herbstamn who was part of an improv group on campus called Mee-ow. So yeah, he was fun and funny. He went on to Second City and is now a legit actor and I hadn't thought of him in a long time before I sat down to write this and then went down a rabbit hole of Mee-ow history. Lotta familiar names to everyone (Seth Myers, Julia Louis Dreyfus) and to me (Paul was in the band, Chickpea and Melissa worked on staff and crew).

Willard could be the subject of a million stories in itself. Freshman year, my friend Fred suggested I run for President. And I did. And I won the election. It was the first time I had ever run for anything. Also the first speech I ever gave. Two hundred ninety-two people lived in Willard and most of them showed up for the elections. I had some rough notes on a small piece of paper and just went for it. Many of my friends also ran for the executive board or one of the floor representatives. All-in the dorm government was about 30 people and had a decent-sized budget to play with. Running that was quite a challenge for a freshman but I got through it with help from friends and mentors.

Willard hosted social events, events with a more academic (loosely defined) focus and even offered actual classes through the University. This was due to its status as a Residential College, which meant we had faculty advisors and mentors. That's how I met people like Classics professors Carl Petry and Dan Garrison. Or Bill Anthony, who taught the Willard Folklore class, where we learned techniques of oral history by recording Willard's illustrious/notorious alumni.

It's also how I became more acquainted with Shep Shanley, the director of undergraduate admissions, whose 50-year career only recently ended. To commemorate his service, Willardites pitched in for a plaque in his honor. I went to the dedication and got a tour of the massive renovation that happened to the building. The plaque hangs in a new common room that is essentially where the room where I lived for two years (121) used to be.

Shep came up to me at a faculty barbecue early in my presidency. He approached me and asked if I was the new president. I asked why he thought so and he said, "you just seem to be in charge," which was a vote of confidence that was much needed and has stayed with me all these years.

One event we hosted featured a Willard alumna and accomplished photographer, Lydia Clarke. She was an actress and traveled the world taking photographs, which were published in leading magazines and shown in galleries. Since many of the images were quite foreign (literally) to their audiences, she stressed the importance of well-written captions.

I'm paraphrasing from memory, but she said something along the lines of, "If a picture alone is worth 1,000 words, imagine the power of a picture plus 100 words."

Her husband was also a pretty well known Northwestern alumnus, actor Charlton Heston. He tagged along and introduced her in that famous voice of Moses from *The Ten Commandments*. I got his autograph as he passed through the lobby, but someone (cough, my eldest) tore it in half when she was young. In retrospect, I should have had Lydia sign something too on the way out.

As someone who is both a photographer and a writer, thinking about the power of combining those things through photos and captions or other surrounding text struck a chord. Lou Reed always was credited as "words and music by Lou Reed," and I adapted that to "words and images by Matt Carmichael."

There are several forms of privilege here. One, the honor and privilege of being able to lead Willard for a year, joining a long tradition of zaniness. Two, the privilege of attending someplace like Northwestern, where I got to have run-ins with all kinds of folks like comedian Denis Leary, or Princess Diana(!), or civil rights leader Jesse Jackson, or Paul Simon (the Senator) or Lydia Clarke Heston and her date. And I mean that in all the different facets of privilege.

Even so, it was impossible to take advantage of all of the opportunities. But also important to take advantage of as many as possible. True then as it is now.

MY MAKERS
ON THE THINGS WE ACQUIRE AND THE CONNECTIONS WE MAKE

As you've been reading, I like meeting the people behind the music, or writing, or other kinds of creative work. Between fandom and my job I've been able to make a lot of opportunities to do so. So far I've written about a lot of rock stars and celebrities. But I have other kinds of heroes. Including some that will expose me for being an odd amalgam of nerdinesses. So this chapter is a bit of a confession about one of those spheres.

As of this writing, the U.S. has imposed tariffs on Mexico and Canada (and most of the rest of the world in a let's say "fluid" manner). Whatever your politics, you likely agree that a policy like that should help U.S. businesses, and I have Ipsos data to support that. But that's not the only outcome. Take Dearborn Denim, a Chicago-based manufacturer of jeans and other apparel. It faces daily challenges in its quest as a small U.S.-based manufacturer: how to sell and market its products, how to deal with lulls or sudden rushes of orders, how to balance the desire to make new products with the need to stock classics and favorites, etc. They source most of their materials in the U.S. but it's not easy. There aren't many cotton mills left in the U.S. making denim. They're able to source all their cotton denim domestically, but they import their stretch denim from... Mexico. It gives them a really small and tight supply chain. Until tariffs.

When the tariffs were levied, the company, like many larger businesses, announced it would try to eat the cost increases as long as it could. That cut its tight margins so it could keep its promise to its customers of quality jeans, at an affordable price while also providing quality jobs in the community.

I have a lot of respect for trying to keep the cost from being passed on. But also, they shouldn't have to be in that position.

I met its CEO, Rob McMillan, during a public tour of their factory, a short drive from my house. I took my family and we got to see where the jeans and belts and shirts are made. It's all on one factory floor from cutting to washing and packing. Every station provides a good job for someone in my community. I have a lot of respect for that too.

Caring about where my jeans are made (and I wear jeans most days, now) is an offshoot of caring about where the things I carry with me are made, as well as the bags that I carry that stuff in. I prioritize companies that make things domestically for economic benefit and a little national pride. But it has the side benefit that I can potentially meet the people who literally make the things. These are some quick stories of meeting these creators and makers.

There's a name for all of this stuff: everyday carry. You can read a really exhaustive version of this story, but it's probably a little much. It was written to share with the EDC community. Because of course there is one. And if there's a "leader" of this community, most people would say it's Taylor Welden. You'll meet him shortly.

What follows are some stories of meeting some of the people who made some of my things. It's probably worth noting some of the things I carry:

- A space pen
- A small microblade from WESN. (I also have an amazingly-left-handed Swiss Army knife, but it's a little big to carry with me).

- A Bellroy wallet (though less frequently now because I have a Bellroy phone case with a card holder built in), which I'm glad to have had replaced after my old wallet and I parted company. That's a "meeting" story of a different sort.
- And if I have my Tom Bihn backpack, I'm carrying a bunch of other stuff. Including a blade-less, TSA-approved multi-tool, because you never know when you'll need a screwdriver. Speaking of my backpack...

TOM BIHN

Making a pilgrimage in Seattle

I coveted the Tom Bihn Synapse 25 backpack for quite some time. And by that I mean that I spent a lot of time thinking about and researching what would be my perfect pack. Turns out two friends and neighbors had the same pack. So although I couldn't go to a store to try one out I could talk to them and see theirs. When I finally ordered mine, one of the online reviews mentioned that they would decorate the shipping boxes if requested. I did, of course. Kat, a worker there, drew adorable little robots and enclosed a hand-written note. Years later on a trip to Seattle, I finally got to see where my bag was made. The factory store is right in the factory, so you can see the people sewing and cutting and crafting as you check out the goods. And who should greet me at the door, but Kat. Personal touches.... It's not just a thing; it's all the things.

FIELD NOTES

I love the idea of Field Notes. I just, um, don't love the form factor of their usual notebooks. It doesn't really work for me. But then they worked with a well-known journalist to make a proper reporters notebook and I now stop in a couple of times a year at Field Notes' HQ to restock. It's handy that they're another Chicago-based manufacturer. When you are there in person you can shop old and rare releases, and you always walk out with a free pencil, notebook and sticker. I've met a few of their staff, one of whom did me, my kids and their classmates a pretty massive solid. Good people, making good stuff. On one visit, I noticed that their cobranded Fisher Space Pen (another American-made product) was essentially left-handed – in that if you are holding the pen in your left hand, the logo is right side up. You, as a (statistically probable) righty, have never noticed that this is rare because your pens are always right side up. But I noticed immediately and then had to pick one up. I was chatting with Bryan whom I met on a store visit and he, the pen's designer, had never noticed or been told that.

PATRICK AYOUB, DETROIT WATCH CO.

Since my first Timex and later a series of Casio Databanks, I've always liked watches. And in adulthood I've wanted, but resisted, a true grownup watch. I did get a Shinola at their factory store. I went with my dad and my son on what I think was my last adventure with my dad. I will always cherish that watch, partially because three generations of Carmichael men were there to buy it.

But Shinola, despite its Detroit roots, is almost a big company now.

I've kept my eye out for something smaller and a little more unique. For me, that turned out to be the 313 area code watch from Detroit Watch Co. It's a throwback design to a rotary phone dial. The leather bracelet has copper-colored stitching to evoke phone wires. As a futurist, I especially enjoyed the irony of having a timepiece that in itself was several kinds of anachronism. Watches themselves are a bit of a throwback, and one that hearkens back to a technology as formerly ubiquitous but now obsolete as a rotary phone was just too perfect. That, and it looks so darn cool. It comes in a variety of area codes, and I thought having a 312 (Chicago's prime area code) would allow me to tie it to both places I've called home.

Each watch is hand assembled by its designer, Patrick Ayoub. I emailed him a perhaps odd question. We wound up speaking by phone about my order. Among other things, he let me choose the serial number. I picked the number that marks the year I left 313 and became a 312 resident. My timepiece therefore bridges the two phases of me.

I asked if I could pick it up in person as I would be in the Detroit area for my high school reunion. He not only agreed but it turned out I would be picking it up at his house. It was basically down the street from where I grew up.

We chatted about watches and Detroit. He told me that the success of his little watch company led Shinola to make an automatic movement for the first time. He told me how hard it was to get packaging in the US and how he had reached out to Defy among others about creating a watch roll for him. And once again I got to shake the hand of someone who made something important to me.

CHRIS TAG, DEFY MANUFACTURING

All of this started with the Defy Square. A friend had one of these bags, and the Cobra buckles caught my eye. He told me about Defy, a local Chicago company. I was intrigued. Down a rabbit hole I went.

When I started reading about Defy and its story I was sold. A guy, Chris Tag, had had enough of the advertising industry and set out to start his own small business. It was a struggle, but eventually took off. They made everything by hand in Chicago. The early bags, like mine, used reclaimed materials like military tarps, seat belts and bike tire tubes. And those buckles. AustriAlpin Cobras. Something like $30 a piece, but they'll never fail. That's something you can, and many have, bet your life on. Later they started making use of another local legend, Horween Leather, from a family-owned tannery nearby.

I love a good brand narrative or story. And I love the idea of small companies with real people making stuff with well-sourced, carefully chosen materials and pure passion. I spent too much time checking out their stuff. Watching for sales. Weighing options. My wife said I wasn't cool enough for the Square, so I settled on the First Class. A messenger. My book was coming out. It'd been a hard and stressful time and I felt like I'd earned a reward. I wanted something unique. Something that was a tool. Something that would last. My wife didn't entirely get my obsession, but supported the idea anyway and got it for me for my birthday.

I loved the look of the First Class, and confirmed that its front pocket could squeeze in my iPad mini. But it was missing something I liked in my current messenger. It lacked a back pocket to stash a magazine or some papers for easy access on the train or plane. Some of Defy's other bags had something like that so I reached out on Facebook and asked if they could put a pocket on a First Class. That's the beauty of small business craftspeople. They agreed and I was sold. I picked it up in person and met Chris himself.

Even more amazing was when a couple of years later, after many miles had been logged on that bag, I reached out again and asked for another mod. The bag had D-rings on the front, which added to the visual badassery of the bag, but functionally meant that anything that you hung from them wasn't covered by the flap. I asked if they could put one on the inside that I could hang my keys on and have them protected. Again, they agreed and I took the bag into the shop. Chris was there and was proud to see one of his earlier designs return with some well-earned patina. I watched as he sewed it in, and met one of the other seamstresses and thus shook the hands that created this thing. Figured I should also pick up a Defy keychain I'd been coveting — with some of that pure Horween goodness. All the better to clip on my new ring.

ROB MCMILLAN, DEARBORN DENIM

As I mentioned earlier, Dearborn Denim makes high quality, reasonably priced jeans and makes them a few miles from my house. Rob, its CEO and founder, used to be in finance but wanted to change gears. I started buying their jeans in 2018 or so. They have struggled a bit here and there. Opened and closed retail locations due to the pandemic. Had a hard time moving their factory to expand. Now, maybe tariffs, too.

They're quite human about everything, including their marketing and the way they run the business. For instance, when they moved their factory they only moved it a mile away, so as not to inconvenience their staff of cutters and sewists with an uprooted commute.

By 2023 they were all up and running in their new space, so they restarted their occasional factory tours. The tours are given by Rob himself. I brought my family and hopefully the kids got a feel for what hand-crafted looks like and how small a supply chain can be. Meeting Rob was fun and I did what I often do, asked in-person for an interview later.

When I interviewed him for *WTF*, we talked about the global economy and the role of Made in the U.S.A in it. He said something that kind of sums up how I feel, too. He said, "I think it's okay to say as an American, I prefer to support jobs in the USA, I align with this person more just by living in the same area as them."

| Rob McMillan giving a tour of the Dearborn Denim Factory

TAYLOR WELDEN
ON PASSIONS AND COMMUNITIES AND FINDING YOUR PEOPLE

In the previous chapter I talked about everyday carry and how I've met some of the makers whose products I deeply appreciate. I mentioned that if the community had a leader it would be Taylor Welden. Welden runs Carryology.com and helps lead the Facebook community that grew out of it. It's a community that seems to thrive uniquely online. I say that partially because many of the brands are online-only, selling directly to buyers. Related to that challenge, there is only one place where you can find a physical store that carries these brands in one place. It's called Suburban and is located in Hong Kong. Amazingly, I had a chance to go make a pilgrimage there during a lay-over on my China trip. It was... not easy to find.

But anyway, Taylor grew Carryology.com into a thriving Web site. The community it fosters is an interesting one in that there are folks from all over the world and all over the political spectrum. There are likely some odd overlaps in the Venns of their interests. But they come together to talk about... well, buying stuff. And like the Bullet Journal community, some seem to just be in it for the consumerism of it all. But some really just want to make sure they get the best stuff for their money because wallets, knives, bags, and pens can last a long time and yeah, you can have a sense of pride about the things you carry. Ipsos data shows that a growing majority like to buy things from brands that match their values. But also that value itself matters, too.

Taylor is an interesting cat, full of personality and a larger-than-life stature. I think that's part of the reason he and this community succeeded. It's not a cult of personality at all. But he's out there leading the life, using the gear he writes about and sharing it and a bit of brotherhood with everyone. (It's certainly not male-only, this space, but leans that way, see the overlapping Venns.) Taylor is an award-winning beard grower, a world traveler and a photographer. At heart, though, he's a designer.

We failed to meet up in person despite both being in the same convention center once (for very different events – his was about textiles, mine market research). But I was able to interview him for *What the Future* and chat for some time about this thing we both care about.

One of the stories he told me was about his trip to Suburban. I was able to work an edited version into the WTF piece, but I'll pull it out here. It was about how fascinating it is that a niche group of people can be super passionate about something, and other folks will buy the stuff even if they're not super passionate about it. We care an awful lot about a thing that nobody else cares about.

Yes, I've gotten comments from other Tom Bihn fans from time to time when I'm wearing my backpack. But that's because we see each other in a sea of people who don't otherwise notice.

We do like to have others to nerd out about this stuff with, which is where the community comes into play. The Facebook group has spawned in-person meet-ups around the world. I went to a Chicago one out of curiosity. It was a fun swap-meet sort of vibe. But I find that "I like backpacks" is a harder jumping off point to build a lasting friendship or deeper relationship with than "I like Poi Dog Pondering," for instance. Maybe it's that bands, through their lyrics and music, tend to draw a slightly more like-minded following? At least for smaller bands? I'm not sure I agree with this even as I type it, thinking specifically of the Metallica/Five Finger Death Punch show I witnessed.

But the Venns are so broad in the Carryology community that maybe it's hard to overlap. Or maybe we're not just bag geeks but also a little bit geek geek, so it's hard to bust through all of that introversion in an afternoon meet-up. Heh.

What's a little different about this is that fandom, unlike, say, collecting Precious Moments figurines, is that everybody owns this stuff. Everyone has pens or pocketknives, or flashlights, and backpacks, satchels, slings etc. to carry them in. Most just don't think about these things very much. It's kind of like cars in that way. Some just buy a box to drive around in. Some really care what's under the hood.

I asked Taylor about this and he agreed wholeheartedly. "Exactly," he said. "Our community will research every material and zipper component. But someone else will just buy the bag because it's cool looking."

And then he told me this story: "I was at Suburban [in Hong Kong], and there was a well-dressed woman in her 50s or 60s. She's grabbing backpacks. She just picks them up, spins around. If I'm interested in a backpack, I'll research every single thing about it for weeks. She was just choosing a backpack based on feel and look and weight. She grabbed an Evergoods bag, and I went over to her and said, 'Oh, this is a good one. My friend owns this company.' She just, like, looked at me. She wasn't rude, but she's like, 'Why are you talking to me about buying a backpack?'"

TED ALLEN
ON FILLING VOIDS

Back in the day, a young editor at *Chicago Magazine* hosted a thing called Journalist Happy Hour. It was exactly what you would think it was. A networking or just war-story-swapping gathering of people who worked in the then-robust Chicago news world. Rivalries were replaced with revelry as folks from the *Tribune* mixed (drinks) with reporters from the *Sun-Times*, *Crain's*, WBEZ and an assortment of local TV, Radio, print and even online people. The host was low-key cool. A good connector who built something valuable. I always enjoyed attending and I met some great people along the way.

Then the host, Ted Allen (yeah, that Ted Allen), moved to New York to take a job at Esquire. That led to his big pivot and break, becoming the food guy on the first seasons of *Queer Eye for the Straight Guy*. Chicago's a big place. You can do great things here. Yet it turned out that Ted's drive and talent were bigger than that. He needed to scale up to New York. But we knew him, *when*.

However, that was it. No more happy hour.

Fast forward a few years and I missed the happy hours. Also the Chicago journalism community needed it more than ever. Things were starting to unravel. So I buckled up and decided to revive it myself.

But then again, I only know who I know. But I knew someone who also knew other people. I pinged Scott Smith. Scott was another member – and better-connected – of the community. I knew his Twitter feed and we'd interacted on that platform for a while. Eventually I made the bold suggestion that we grab lunch sometime and meet in person. You can do that and make a virtual friend a real friend.

Over lunch, I suggested we revive the happy hour. Between us we would know enough folks. We put together a list. Suggested they bring friends. And we made a thing.

For the record, I emailed Ted and asked for his blessing to carry on. Of course he thought it was a great idea.

Scott and I evolved it slightly. In addition to a nice gathering, off-the-record, we invited guests. We had friends who were doing cool things for the city, and other organizations that were interested in or of interest to journalists. They would talk about whatever they wanted, but not for very long. And then we all went back to drinking. This is a favorite format of mine, to this day.

We also used these events to make new friends. You'll meet one of them later.

Over the years, I've done this again and again in different ways. I've created advisory boards. I've created group chats. I started a networking group at *Crain's* for its 40 Under 40s. I've put together urbanists, futurists, business leaders and more. A few things happen:

They all get to meet each other. Interesting people working on interesting things. That's…. huge. And powerful. They get to have those connections from then on. Everybody learns from each other. I get to meet everyone. That's a fascinating place to be, because by default I wind up in the room, too.

Be a connector. Everybody wins, and learns and grows. Building communities is a super power. But it's not one that takes super strength. Or even money. Just be curious. Be friendly. Give people interesting problems that they will want to solve. Fill voids. Taylor Welden built a great community of otherwise disparate folks with a single common, niche interest. I guess I have, too.

I couldn't have built any of these communities with only the people I knew as a starting point. Choose your friends and your partners wisely. As I keep saying, surround yourself with interesting people. If you give interesting people interesting projects, they'll want to get involved. I think Scott would agree that's what happened here.

Hopefully, when you build them, others will pick up the torch when you're ready to pass it on. But even if not, everyone involved got to meet some new people.

That's pretty great in itself.

Now I think it's time to meet arguably the best example of this, Richard Florida.

RICHARD FLORIDA
ON GIVING INTERESTING PEOPLE INTERESTING CHALLENGES

Richard Florida and I are sitting at a bar, eating pizza. We're in Toronto, where he teaches at the University. 'Teaches' is an understatement. He has his own Institute. But for now, we're eating and talking about cities and music, two of our favorite topics. I got extremely lucky and happened to be in town on a night when his family was already at his winter home in Miami and the class he was teaching was winding down so when I shot him a "hey, I'm going to be in town" dart he was actually available.

Richard Florida was once aptly described as "the closest an urbanist will ever get to being a household name." He would beg to differ and suggest Jane Jacobs, one of *his* heroes and mentors. But he is known for coining an idea of a "creative class" of people and their importance to cities. This idea helped spark a renaissance and remaking of many of the world's cities, large and small.

I was first introduced to his work when I was writing about stats and demographics at *AdAge*. I then interviewed him for the blog I started there and again at *Crain's Chicago*.

When I started at *Livability* I knew I had a daunting challenge. We wanted to be known as THE authority on best places to live. But we weren't yet known for anything.

I figured we needed a partner. I didn't know who that should be, but I knew Richard would know and that an introduction from him to whomever would go a long way.

However, Richard Florida is a busy guy. I knew he was hosting a conference in Miami and so I bought a ticket and got on a plane.

I had a big ask of him and figured it would be better done in person. Sure enough, I was able to track him down. At this point, I'd met him once before, briefly, in New York (when I also met Joel Kotkin and Dan Ariely), but I was pleasantly surprised that he remembered me and knew who I was.

I told him my interesting challenge: I wanted to do the best Best Places list possible. I knew this was a topic he cared about a lot, having written *Who's Your City*.

I then asked him my favor: Could he introduce me to someone who could help me figure out how do that? What happened next literally changed the course of my career and life.

He said, "Why don't you go to Toronto and meet with my team. We'd be happy to help." So the intro he made wasn't to someone else, exactly. It was to his own researchers! I was floored at the generosity and the curiosity.

This also fit a pattern which leads to the three lessons of this meeting. The first is that you need to be ready to make the big ask. But I also knew I had the second lesson going for me: Give interesting people interesting problems and they tend to want to help you solve them. I had an interesting problem: how to create a credible "best places to live" list. Richard, and later his team, were filled with curiosity. They wanted to solve the problem and thereby help me solve it.

And part of that is the third lesson. Believe in the power of your story. I had a solid story to tell, about how we wanted to do this project right and wanted to have a partner who could help us. And how we wanted to do it right for the right reasons. People needed better data about places and a better understanding of what makes a good place vs. what people think makes a good place. Richard knew that. And again, wanted to help.

I didn't even have a current passport! But I got one and headed up to Toronto and met with Kevin, Zara and the rest of the team who would become excellent collaborators. I got to return the favor ever so slightly when Kevin visited Chicago and I was able to introduce him to Ken Waagner and a charity he was working with at the time, which oddly meant I wound up having a chat with the two of them and the charity's main backer, Luke Walton. Of the Walton family. Like, the Walmart Waltons. But I digress.

In the end, Richard was gracious. His team helped me build an index of livability that carried on long after I left *Livability*. It's built through partnerships with data providers, many of whom became friends along the way. All curious, all eager to help solve this problem.

Lending his credibility did indeed help Livability.com establish its own, which helped me establish my own. In short, I owe Richard a lot.

Interviewing Richard Florida in Nashville, before he ditched me to go hang out with Jack White, which, fair.

Later he was my first interview as I built the first issue of *What the Future* at Ipsos. I knew that if I was going to talk about the future of cities, Richard was the guy I wanted to talk to.

MEETING MY HEROES

Beyond that, I knew that if he would agree to it, anyone else I approached to interview would realize that if Richard Florida was in, then what I was doing was legit and they would agree, too. Thus *WTF* was born and I owe Richard now two entire careers.

I later enrolled in a certificate program about Placemaking and Economic Development Richard set up at his other academic appointment, NYU. It was taught with his colleague Stephen Pedigo, another curious collaborator I've now worked with over the years as well.

More recently, when I was in Toronto and met up with Richard, he gave me a bunch of recommendations for places to eat and a great walking tour, because of course he loved to tout the best things about his city and why, for him and many others, it was a Best Place to Live. My boss at the time, Anne, and I really enjoyed the walking tour and seeing the city through his eyes.

I can't say enough good things about Richard, his ideas, and his generosity in sharing them and his time.

But again, it all comes down showing up, finding good partners, telling good stories. Oh yeah, and then carrying it all through. *Livability*'s list was one that got the site a lot of attention and clicks, which was great. However the best praise was from the mayors of the towns we talked about. They understood we had done the work and that our list wasn't merely click-bait. That led to a lot more conversations, which I'll get to next.

THE NEW URBANISTS
ON SETTING YOUR OWN CURRICULUM IN LIFE

As mentioned, I'm a believer that a great way to learn is to read books. People who know a lot about a thing put all of the best things they know in one, small, usually digestible format. Whatever the topic, someone has written a book about it.

Being a journalist grants me an amazing super power. When I'm done with the book, I can often call up the ~~teacher~~ author and ~~have office hours~~ interview them for a story.

When I started at *Livability*, it was a new field for me. I'd been reading and writing about demographics and touched on urban planning issues at *AdAge* (reading books and interviewing the likes of Richard Florida, Ed Glaeser and Greg Lindsay), but the idea of what makes a place a great place to live was a much broader topic.

I needed to get up to speed, quickly, so I devised a plan. I would read the key books. I would do the research and the work. Much as I had at *AdAge*, I would start a blog so I had a place to write about these topics as I read about them. The blog would also be a place I could post interviews with the authors of the books. Finally, because I knew this would be an ongoing thing, I would set up an advisory board for *Livability* with as many of these people as I could. The idea being that I could use that to create ongoing relationships with key people, and hopefully feed them some research, too.

I got a lot of great people on the advisor board: Joel Kotkin; Kevin Stolarick, who was Richard Florida's lead researcher; economist Jed Kolko; and Emily Rose-Talen, Jeff Speck and Ellen Dunham-Jones, founding members of the Center for New Urbanism. The CNU was a group of urban theorists and planners who had really figured out how to design great communities. Some I would later meet at conferences. All of them I would interview for the *Livability* Blog. You can still read a lot of these interviews which I now host at www.bestplacesto.live.

I learned important lessons about process and about having the right people at the table. One of the leaders of the New Urbanism movement, Emily Rose-Talen, noted that most of the New Urbanist leaders were architects. She thought they needed more policy people, too, to help take design into reality. Lynn Richards, who at the time headed the Congress of the New Urbanism, talked about how much policy is local, but that it's often simpler to work at the state level. As she said, "There are 75,000 units of local government and there are 50 states." I learned more and more about why policy of all kinds matters so much, and how policy all interconnects. Transportation policy and zoning policies and housing policies and environmental policies and anti-poverty and anti-racism policies are all the same thing in many ways. Which can be problematic in the U.S. because we have focused on the wrong things for so long.

I talked to New Urbanist pioneer and walkability expert, Jeff Speck. He literally wrote the book on it (*Walkable City*). He told me, "The way we subsidize things and don't subsidize others favors Americans making the wrong choices. We encourage people to live in this country in terms of their housing and transportation choices. I don't want you to get your unsustainable life more cheaply than someone else's more sustainable life."

Speck went on to talk about the worst kind of development model, yet one so dominant in the U.S.: sprawl. He said, "Most of sprawl is unfixable. Almost any city built before World War II, if it has any economic growth whatsoever, has a downtown that is ready to come back to life if it hasn't already. If we're interested in growing into the 21st century in a sustainable way, our governments at every scale need to create programs that make it easier for people to move to those places to live and work instead of into sprawl."

Elizabeth Plater-Zyberk (yup, another New Urbanist) taught me about sprawl, too. She literally wrote the book on it, (*Suburban Nation: The Rise of Sprawl and the Decline of the American Dream*). She told me, "The U.S. really is the exemplar of sprawl. The idea of everyone having a lot of space, of everyone getting an automobile and having a certain amount of financial leverage, which didn't exist in other parts of the world – and still does not, by the way – really supported that type of growth."

She, too, talked about policy. "It's government's role to help coordinate the individual efforts. You get out of the way of some things and then you try to make some things happen. In a sense, when it comes to cities, government is a developer."

Many of the people I talked to weren't just idealists. They were pragmatic. They realized we live in a capitalist country. Policy is important, but one way to effectively convince policy leaders is through economic arguments. As Richards told me, "The issue isn't to demonize the people who still want your single-family detached home out in the middle of nowhere, but rather to say, 'If 50% of the population want a walkable, livable space and the market is only responding with 5% or 6%, there's still a significant gap and that's the gap we're addressing."

I learned a lot quickly, and would and still do read and think a lot about what makes a great place. The list I built, with help from Richard Florida's team and Ipsos and so many other partners, was, in my not-so-humble-opinion, the most rigorous and defensible list of Best Places.

Yet after all of my research, all of the surveys, all of the interviews, all of the spreadsheets. I boiled it all down to one slide:

Great cities should be places where you can LIVE.

L stood for Level: Cities create an even playing field so all residents can afford to take part in the city's offerings.
I stood for Inclusive: Cities exemplify diversity not just by race and ethnicity, but age, income and experience.
V stood for Variety: Cities should offer options for all facets of life, from housing to healthcare, to amenities.
E stood for Engaged: Residents are out and about helping create the community, which truly matters in a great place.

When I was traveling around to places like Bend, Oregon and Boise, Idaho giving talks in various communities about how they could become more livable places, I would make a joke that I really wanted to use Choice instead of Variety but that LICE wasn't a very good acronym.

One person I interviewed didn't think it was all that useful to try to shape policy, at least if you were an individual voter. He was Bill Bishop, author of "The Big Sort," about how America was becoming more geographically polarized. He told me something that's likely true, but still kind of depressing. "It's inefficient to vote to get what you want," he said. "But as places get more different, it becomes very efficient to move to get what you want."

After learning the importance of policy, I then turned my attention to the leaders elected to set it for America's Best Places to Live. Clearly if these cities were successful, they must be doing some things right. It was time to meet the mayors.

THE MAYORS
ON LESSONS LEARNED BY THE THOSE LEADING THE CHARGE

Bruce Katz of the Brookings Institution, in his book *Metropolitan Revolution*, talks about Mayors as people who get stuff done. They have to, he says, because they are the front line. If they don't get the trash picked up, keep the streets safe, and plow the snow, they're done. That last one led to the first (and only) female mayor in Chicago's history, Jane Byrne. Really.

During my time at *Livability* I had the opportunity to meet and/or interview many mayors of cities of all sizes. They were all thoughtful and pragmatic. They came from cities in red states and blue states. Their focus, however, was on making their cities great places to live. The building blocks of livability are a thing that there is largely bipartisan agreement on. I should know, I've been surveying about that for 10+ years now. Sure, they have to deal with politics, but the conversations were never political. They really did just focus on what needed to be done and how to do it.

Oddly the only one I remember turning me down was Oak Park's! Looking back through those interviews, I thought I'd pull out some favorite quotes and lessons and share a few stories of how I met a few of them.

The mayor I had the most contact with over the years is Madison mayor, Paul Soglin. He has a unique perspective on an unusual city. In 2011 he was elected for his third (and final?) stint as mayor, having served in the 1970s and then again from 1989 to 1997. "It's called recidivism," he told me.

I first met him when he reached out to see why Madison hadn't scored higher on our first Top 100 Best Places to Live ranking. He had convened a task force to make specific recommendations about how the city could do better in next year's rankings. They had tried to reverse-engineer our algorithm and had some questions. In answering them, I found an error in our data – someone doing data entry had transposed 'Madison, WI' with 'Madison Heights, MI.' Fixing that landed Soglin's city in the number five slot that first year. He wanted number one, however, because he could see that we'd done the work and he agreed with what we prioritized in our list. He didn't want to be number one just on the list, he wanted to be number one because his city honestly was best at all the things we measured. By the next year, he made it.

Madison itself keeps things challenging because the population is always shifting. It's rare to have a city with a large minority population that's nearly equal parts African-American, Asian and Hispanic -- and each of these segments is growing. Soglin's drive to improve isn't surprising for a mayor whose only regret from his time(s) in office is this: "In my previous tenures I had a 20-year view, which is far longer than most elected politicians. I should have had a 40 year view."

When asked how to make a great city, he told me, "You don't go out there chasing and recruiting companies to leave another city and come to yours. What you do is exactly the notion of what [Livability.com is] trying to evaluate. You build a great place and they will come."

I did get to go visit and have a press conference with him when Madison took the top slot. Since then we've kept in touch. He'll call me out of the blue with Census data questions or to debate various topics. Last time I was in Madison (for a Neil Gaiman reading) we had dinner and talked about cities and about his other great love, baseball. He grew up a Sox fan, which I forgive him for. But has a great and learned perspective on our nation's pastime as well.

He was never afraid to dig into the data. He noticed something weird in the Census data for his city and got the Census Bureau ... not to retract it, they never do that, but to write him a letter saying, essentially "maybe just don't look at that particular stat too closely, OK?" I can't imagine a lot of politicians debating which versions of the American Community Survey are best for which applications. He's wonky, in all the good ways. Much respect.

Pittsburgh's mayor, Bill Peduto, and I had a quick walk-and-talk interview through Chicago. He had to run to his hotel to pick up his bags and head home for a big city council vote he was quarterbacking via text as we walked. He drew a lot of comparisons between his city and my former city, Detroit. Like Soglin, he seemed to see the need to take the long view, and like Madison, Pittsburgh was seeing its old bets pay off.

"During the 1980s [non-profit foundations] kept our heads above the water. What they were doing was investing in long-term approaches and basically at the same time our 'eds and meds' were just beginning their process of coming to the forefront," he said. For Detroit, another flailing Midwestern metropolis coping with its somewhat-post-industrial present, the work is still getting started.

He also talked about immigration as a key to growth. And he talked about developing bike lanes and the importance of strong neighborhood businesses. I suggested he was of the new-school of mayors. "You mean the old school?" he countered. "How do we get back to 1950 with urban neighborhood functions? It's unique businesses, family-owned businesses, a walkable accessible business district where everything is right outside your door... Access to public transit so if you don't want to own a car you don't have to... Affordable housing and access to jobs. It's all those components are 1950 urban America."

Nineteen Fifties urban America was quashed by a lot of

things, not the least of which was a concerted effort by General Motors, Firestone and others to kill the trolley system that existed in most cities because they wanted trolleys replaced with busses using Firestone tires. This was a thing that happened, and led to a landmark court case.

At a CEO for Cities conference, I wound up sitting next to longtime Greenville, S.C., mayor, Knox White, at dinner one night. We had a great chat and I wound up giving him a lift back to his hotel afterwards so we could continue the conversation. When I got to interview him formally he talked about a big project his city undertook in the 1970s to remove a well-traveled roadway and revitalize a river-front area and waterfall it had essentially paved over. It was very controversial at the time. He told me in 2015, "I had someone come up to me yesterday and say 'I used to have a store on Main Street back in the '70s and I was against everything you guys wanted to do and boy was I wrong.' About once a month someone says that to me."

He continued, "Having an urban core that really surprises people is a major economic development tool. We didn't plan it that way, but oh my goodness in terms of recruiting people and companies it's become the biggest thing."

The lesson there is that sometimes things are hard. Sometimes people don't have the vision you do but you have to follow your vision anyway. If you're right, and right for the right reasons — you've done the research, you've thought through the scenarios and you've talked to the right people for ideas — you just have to find a way to get it done. People will come around, and they'll thank you for it later.

That was also the philosophy of Asheville, N.C., mayor, Esther Manheimer. She said, "You can be an auto-pilot city and just provide the basic services, or you can innovate, [be] forward-thinking and you can plan it."

I met two different Grand Rapids mayors. The first was longtime mayor George Heartwell. He told me about the importance of having people invest in your city if you want it to thrive.

Billionaires can be especially helpful, especially if they roll up their sleeves and pitch in, not just write checks. Though checks are helpful, too. "We are very conscious of the fact that Grand Rapids would not be the vibrant city that it is today if it weren't for the fact that a number of people have made their fortunes here and have elected to stay here and raise their families here. They're investing in the city both for economic gain and for philanthropic purposes."

One such family in the Grand Rapids area is the Meijer family. My mom's cousin Harvey Lemmen was their right-hand man as they built out the Super Store chain that bears their name. That might sound like a big claim, but it's quite true. The Meijers donated the funds for a cancer center in his name, and the name of one other longtime Meijer leader. He's also buried in the Meijer family plot at Meijer Gardens, which is about as high on an honor as I can imagine. Harvey himself was also very philanthropic and, until it closed, there was a Planned Parenthood named in his honor, too.

I was invited to put together and moderate a panel of mayors for a conference in northern California and I reached out to Mayor Soglin and thought I'd invite the Grand Rapids mayor, too. It turned out Mayor Heartwell had retired. His successor, the youngest and first female mayor in Grand Rapids history, Rosalynn Bliss, was happy to join. I got to see her do the most Michigan thing ever. Someone asked her where Grand Rapids was, and she held up her hand and pointed to its location using her built-in mitten map.

We stayed in touch and several years later when we traveled as a family to Grand Rapids for my parents' 50th wedding anniversary (they were married there) she issued a proclamation in their honor. She was a big beer fan, so I brought her a gift package from Oak Park's first brewery, Kinslahger, and suggested Oak Park and Grand Rapids should become sister beer cities. Which isn't a thing, but she was open to how it could become a thing. Maybe I should pick that idea back up...

I interviewed Tampa mayor Bob Buckhorn after reading about a project he was doing using data from Foursquare (a platform now called Swarm that I think I'm alone in still using) to learn how people were using and moving around his city. He told me, "From 30,000 feet I was able to look at the heat maps and say 'this is where people are congregating or this is where they're Tweeting from' and that gives me a better feel for where the demand might occur down the road. You look at development patterns – what would be an appropriate use in that vicinity? Is it commercial? Is it retail? Is it residential?" I loved how he was using data to help plan.

There's a funny thing with cities. Even in red states, the cities themselves are often blue. And sometimes the red state governors work against the interests of their own citizens out of ... I don't know. Spite?

Buckhorn told me, "The Obama administration was going to fund $3 billion for high-speed rail – the first in the country – from Orlando to Tampa. The right of way had already been acquired. It would have created 6,000 temporary construction jobs. The governor [Rick Scott] was elected in 2010, about 6 months later, in essence said he wasn't interested and gave the money back to the federal government. I've had the mayor of Detroit thank me because as he said, 'We're taking the money that your governor gave back and we're building our light rail system with it.' There's a little frustration here in Florida about that decision."

That was funny because I'd just been in Detroit reading about how the city had done just that with its Q line, starting to rebuild what was lost in the '50s with the whole Firestone/GM thing. Many of those old trolleys are in the Chicago suburbs now at the Illinois Railway Museum, with warehouses full of cars from midwestern cities, a tragic reminder of all that was lost.

Finally I met Chicago's mayors. I met Mayor Daley by accident while walking through Grant Park with Pam and a very tiny Meredith. Mayor Rahm Emanuel I met a few times, often with my friend Sean who worked for him. I also flew on planes with both of them (separately and in a different class of seats) at various points.

Rahm was wicked smart, and sometimes just wicked. At that event with Bruce Katz I mentioned at the beginning, he also spoke. He was asked about Chicago losing businesses to places like Houston, Texas. He said, water is important. Chicago sits next to one of the largest sources of fresh water in the world. Climate change is real and Texas won't fare well. So yeah, move to Houston or Dallas. "Then try to take a shower in 10 years, and see how that turns out." [Narrator: It didn't even take 10 years.] They'll be back, he said.

Rahm did a thing that seemed funny at the time, but was prescient. He carried wipes in his suit pocket. His job required him to shake a lot of hands and as soon as he was done, he'd disinfect.

That was a long chapter, but covered a lot of ground in time and across America. There are a lot of great ideas and lessons here about building cities. Those lessons apply in just about anything you'd ever want to do for a living. Network, stay focused, use data, think about and plan for the future. Having friends who can support your efforts really helps. Also, love where you live.

Mayors get things done because they have to. Sadly our federal government seems hell-bent currently on not getting useful things done. It's easy to imagine an alternate universe where that's not the case.

Speaking of alternate universes, I was telling a story to the kids I often drive to softball in what has come to be known as "the party van." I realized it would be a perfect fit to include here. It's time to meet not Mayor Emanuel, but @mayoremanuel. Confused? Read on.

THE MAYORS EMANUEL
ON THE POWER OF MAKING "GOOD NIGHTS"

In the history of Twitter, two things stand out to me as the best uses of the platform. These are two instances of people who took advantage of its strengths and did something unique and special. Oddly, I know both dudes involved in these very different uses and both have turned their use cases into books. The first is Andy Carvin, whom I've name-checked here before. He's a friend from college, another of the amazing people who lived in Willard's room 121 at some point. While working at NPR, he used Twitter to report on the Middle East uprising known as Arab Spring. Using the platform to find (and fact check!) on-the-ground sources, he quarterbacked coverage in real-time, and at great personal cost. You can read about it in his book, Distant Witness. Andy probably merits his own chapter here, but I do find it odd to write about people I actually know well. He's since gone on to do heroic work with one of the great challenges of our time: fighting disinformation, which I interviewed him about for *What the Future*.

But today I want to tell the story of the other guy, Dan Sinker. Dan is a Chicago journalist, muckraker, punk chronicler, zine publisher, educator, genre-bender, the Candle King of Kickstarter, and (and this is how I met him) dad. When Rahm Emanuel began his quest to be Chicago's Mayor, Dan started a

Twitter feed called @mayoremanuel. Except no one knew who was behind it at the time. It chronicled a parallel universe to Rahm's actual campaign. There were amazing characters developed like a campaign sidekick duck named Quaxelrod (a nod to Rahm advisor David Axelrod). There were otherworldly plot arcs. People around town, including Rahm himself, speculated about who was behind it, but everyone was talking about the feed and had alerts set up on their phones to let them know when new posts dropped.

It's hard to explain how amazingly epic this story was, and all done when Twitter had its 140-character limit. It made a small corner of the world a better place for a brief moment in time.

The story built to a Sopranos-style crescendo on election night. It was a night that was apocalyptic in so many ways, including the Thunder Snow blanketing the city.

After the election, Rahm offered $5,000 to the charity of @mayoremanuel's choice if he would come forward. Dan Sinker couldn't refuse that and the two met up on WLS. Dan donated it (it was upped to $12,000 I think with some matching donations) to Young Chicago Authors, and its program Louder than Bombs, a non-profit that supported teen poets.

All of this also got pulled into a book. Twitter founder Biz Stone wrote a forward to it.

I went to the book launch party at Chicago's legendary Hideout. It was a crazy mix of people. John Tolva, then the CTO for the City of Chicago DJd. Oh, over there is Harper Reed and a bunch of folks from Obama's campaign tech team. Hey, Cook County commish John Fritchey, how ya doin'...

Dan read from the book, of course. Kids from Louder than Bombs read their poetry. But there were two special guests who kind of stole the show.

One was Rahm Emanuel, himself. Yeah, for real. Pulls up in his mayoral SUV with his security detail. Chats with guests for a while, chats with Dan and splits. Shook some hands, and likely disinfected after.

Dan had a copy of his book for attendees to sign as a guest book, an awesome idea that I later stole for my own book party. Rahm graciously autographed it, with the inscription, "You're an a$$hole."

I caught Rahm on the way out, and since I always have a Sharpie, I asked him to sign my copy, too. So my copy is signed by both mayors.

Mayor Emanuel signing for @MayorEmanuel

But the true highlight comes based on a vignette in the book itself. In real life, Wilco were playing a fundraiser for Rahm. In @MayorEmanuels' universe that came with an unusual string and one singer Jeff Tweedy pushed back on. From the feed:

"Tweedy's being pissy because he doesn't want to play any Black Eyed Peas songs. What the fuck? People love that shit. Not saying they're a good band--they're fucking terrible. But if you want people with money to give that shit away, play the Black Eyed Peas. But no, Tweedy's pulling this fucking 'I'm in Wilco, so I'm going to play Wilco songs' bullshit, like he knows anything about fundraising."

Now, I mentioned that Dan had some roots in the punk scene as the founder of the *Punk Planet* zine. Through it he knew Sue

Miller, the co-owner of Lounge Ax, a venue so special it got its own chapter. She was also... Mrs. Tweedy. So he reached out with a crazy idea, which she loved and passed on and then somehow Jeff Tweedy showed up to play at the book launch. "If you want someone who has an incredible legacy to do something really stupid, the best route is through their spouse," said Dan in the introduction. And, you guessed it, Tweedy came and performed the songs of the Black Eyed Peas, including a strained and yet perfect rendition of "I Gotta Feeling" and a dramatic reading of "My Humps." Sue would email Dan with updates as Tweedy "hilariously" rehearsed in their basement. Please, please watch those videos.

"I'm not saying anything bad about the Black Eyed Peas, I do think, having spent some time with their material, that they are evil geniuses. My children are worried for me, I'm worried for me, my wife is worried for me and I really hope I can get these songs out of my head before I have to tour again," said Tweedy before launching headlong into "Rock that Body."

In the end, the event was covered by NBC, the *Sun-Times* and more but the best recounting is on Scott Smith's blog, of course. NBC's post mentions that Rahm even retweeted a photo of the event. The link to the photo platform that was hosted on is gone now, but I can share the photo here, because the photo Rahm retweeted was *mine!*

MEETING MY HEROES

So yeah, I went to a book signing by the fictional Mayor Emanuel, met him and the real Mayor Emanuel, had them both sign my book and then had the real Mayor retweet my Tweet about the Twitter version of him.

All of this because someone had a creative idea and just went with it. Both Dan and Andy looked at a new platform, looked at what everyone was doing with it and thought, "You know, we can use it better." They made something entirely new possible, and did it with incredible amounts of dedication and passion.

That, my friends, is Chicago. And one of my most favorite Chicago memories.

AMY WEBB
ON THE FUTURE, AND MAKING YOUR OWN

Amy Webb is one of the best-known futurists there is and one of the smartest folks I've ever met, which is saying a lot if you look at all the other names in this section.

She's helped elevate the entire industry and practice of foresight and showcase the role of technology in driving it. Her annual tech trends talk is a must-see at SXSW and was a must-see at the Online News Association all the years she gave it there.

She's incredibly generous with her methods. In addition to writing a book detailing them (*The Signals are Talking*), she open-sources many of her frameworks. She taught workshops at ONA (I was lucky to attend the first one) and now hosts a master class at SXSW. She's a great example of how sometimes the more you give away and the more you give back, the more you get.

Amy has helped people learn how to systematically think about the future, listen to the signals, be ready for any scenario, and also understand that the future is really what you (and others) make it. When I first interviewed her in *WTF* she told me, "Unless you are willing to go to uncomfortable places and to meet that anxiety and fear about change about the future you know then you become shackled by the present. We call that the paradox of the present."

She's also just a darn nice, funny and generous human.

We first met in person at ONA and both had a sense we'd already met and known each other for some time. Those moments are rare, but are also a signal to be listened to.

I ran some questions for her about future thinking on Ipsos Global Advisor, which she used in that ONA talk and we collaborated on a number of things, including her amazing role as a contributor for *What the Future* – long before I would ever feel comfortable wearing the "futurist" title myself, and years before I would attend the Foresight certificate program at University of Houston. Amy's always been an inspiration and mentor, especially as she pivoted from a career in journalism herself.

Hosting Amy Webb (photo: Robert K. Elder)

I've also met so many awesome futurists and friends through her, including Melanie and the rest of her also-whip-smart team. During the pandemic, they hosted a series of weekly calls she described as "like pick-up basketball games, but for futurists." We'd start our weeks talking about all the things we saw going on in the world and the signals we were hearing.

Those calls were magic and inspiring, and in their absence I've tried to build some communities myself, much like I did with Journalist Happy Hour.

There are all kinds of reasons for her not to be generous with her time. Or not to be a great connector. Or not to give back to building up the profession and helping the world understand that it *needs* to plan for the future, and more importantly that it *can* plan for the future if it puts in the work.

But she leans into all of the reasons *why* instead of *why not* and makes things better because of it.

THE FUTURISTS
ON THE IMPORTANCE OF UNDERSTANDING THE FUTURE

I never went to SXSW when it was primarily a music festival and I was a concert photographer and rock reviewer. It sounded like a lot of hassle and late nights and all of the bands I wanted to see played Metro the week before or after anyway. I was cheap and lazy and liked sleeping – all of which were bad qualities for a concert photographer and rock reviewer. But I also had a bit of regret and FOMO.

Later, it added an interactive festival when I was covering online things and I still didn't go because I didn't have anyone who would pay to send me. I had more FOMO because now I could follow along on Twitter and see in real time all the things I was missing. In 2009, my Facebook status was "is not at SXSW," which offered no context but was either defiant or expressing that FOMO or maybe a little of both.

Finally, as a futurist, I got to go, starting in 2022, when it was first reopening after the pandemic. What changed? One thing was that my heroes shifted. My current heroes all were going to SXSW so it was time for me to go, too.

Straight off the plane I ducked into Amy Webb's annual tech trends session (one of the biggest draws of the conference, which in a normal year has an enormous line that starts hours beforehand), and walked right in and sat on the floor on the side. You could get into anything because there was only 30% of the usual attendance. I got to see Amy's talk for the first time live and meet much of her awesome team in person for the first time. And I got to meet lots of other futurists and future-thinkers.

I was in a new space and needed to meet new people and build a new network.

SXSW is a place where it pays to get over my introversion. I talk to people I'm walking near. I talk to the people sitting around me in the sessions. There are so many interesting folks from so many different walks of life and careers. Oh, you work for the sovereign fund of Norway which controls 1.8 trillion in assets? That's cool. And you build instructions for the chips that are running all the AI? Sweet. You're trying to figure out how we can communicate with other species? Ok, that's rad. You write video games? Dude.

In the first two years I went I saw talks by (and later met) Rohit Bhargava and Ian Beacraft (whom Tracy Schmidt thought I should meet, and I'm glad she did). They would both become friends and collaborators. Ian is a brilliant mind and fantastic presenter. Rohit is those things too, and also an impressive collector of interesting people. I admire them both for their drive and their generosity.

I watched Pete Buttigieg give a master class in how to hold a town hall. I saw internet heroes like Neal Stephenson and Bruce Schneier. And heard/met a trove of people who had already or would eventually wind up in the pages of *WTF* like Taryn Southern and Douglas Rushkoff. I asked questions during Q&A (following my personal rule that everyone should follow: Less preamble, more actual question, the mic in the audience doesn't mean you're now a speaker.) I chatted with presenters after their panels, which, as a speaker myself, I know speakers honestly appreciate. I learned that the featured speakers on the big ballroom stages are often doing six other things at SXSW over the course of the conference where they are more approachable.

I chatted with other people who asked interesting questions

during Q&A, which is how I met and befriended Annie Hardy. I wandered through the VR exhibit and chatted with the people making amazing new things in amazing new media like AR, VR and XR. That's how I met Cameron Kostopoulos, who was experimenting with storytelling, and technology and empathy around issues of gender and transgender/genderqueer topics.

I also just ran into people from other parts of my life who were drawn to this place, too. Sometimes that was deliberate, like meeting folks in person I'd interviewed in *WTF*. Love that. Especially if where we wind up meeting up is a small party with Paris Hilton as the DJ, because it's SXSW after all and these things happen. Or chance encounters with college-era friends I hadn't seen in ages.

Then I did two things that are my favorite things. First, I followed up. I didn't single-serve-friendship these folks. I tried to keep those interactions going. Second, I found ways to introduce these folks to each other and either expand existing communities or build new ones. That's the most "everybody wins" outcome possible.

All of this set me up for 2025. After three years (attending twice) of building networks and learning how SXSW works and pitching (unsuccessfully) a talk, I joined a group of these new SXSW friends doing something new. Annie, Ian, Alex Whittington and I debuted a new, fun-but-relevant format for thinking about the future: Foresight Improv.

I got to share the stage with three incredibly smart polymaths who also happen to be fun, funny, kind and thoughtful futurists. We talked about 18 audience-chosen "future of..." topics in an hour. Some we pre-seeded but didn't know which ones the audience would vote up. Some, the audience suggested when they came in, on index cards we pulled out of Annie's rhinestone cowboy hat. We did a broad range including the future of war, thinking, vacation and even toilet paper. I also took on one of the most popular suggestions: democracy.

I asked the audience if they wanted 'dystopian' or 'utopian' and they chose 'dystopian.' I talked about how the currency of democracy is trust and participation and we're lacking in both of those. I didn't go too dark, however. And then I did the last suggestion which was about radio stations playing music, during which I talked about KEXP and my WTF interview with John in the Morning. of course.

In addition, I helped launch a report I'd worked on for quite some time at Ipsos with our partner, the Global Futures Society, who brought their Museum of the Future to SXSW (with an awesome Refik Anadol installation, another awesome person I'd interviewed for *WTF*.) I taped a podcast talking about it and finding all about how futurists view the world, and how that differs from how everyone else does.

And then I did all the things I do to keep building. I met cool people I was sitting next to in sessions, like Adrianne and Cheryl. I reconnected with folks from past lives, like Tim from the Polyphonic Spree and his crew. I chatted with speakers after their talks, like Scott Galloway. I hung out with people I had met virtually but never gotten to spend time with, like Sarah and Joana, and we all introduced each other to new people. And I reconnected with my SXSW friends whom I'm in more frequent touch with but either met or mostly see at SXSW like Amy, Rohit, Ian and Annie.

In most cases, I followed some advice from my high school English teacher, Dr. Welch, who told students to "get a seat in the front row, up close to the action." That was not a lesson I took to heart in high school, but he was right and I listened...eventually.

I also had the most SXSW experience possible:

I'm walking from my hotel and the guy next to me is wearing a flight suit. He could be in a band with a gimmick, sure. But no, a glance to the side and I catch a glimpse of a NASA patch. Then a fleet of cars goes by advertising HOKA shoes. The cars say "Fly Human Fly." This is a sign, clearly, partially because I'm wearing a stylish and super comfy pair of shoes HOKA's sister Deckers Brands brand AHNU sent me (cf WTF Influence!). So I turn to the guy and say, "I guess some humans fly more than others." I tell him I can't quite see his name tag, but I'm assuming....He chuckles and introduces himself as A NASA TEST PILOT. It's Nils Larson! We chat, and as we're walking we meet a teacher from the U.K. whose students have made mock NASA mission patches and he gives each of us one (they were adorable). And then another guy comes up and introduces himself as the NASA guy making the cameras they're sending to the moon. This is all within a block or two.

I wound up interviewing Nils, Cathy Bahm (who is the project manager for the X59 program) and Larry Cliatt (who is NASA's "Sonic Boom guy.").

That was my third SXSW in a nutshell. I crushed it.

Then I hopped on my flight home.

The captain came on and asked us all to remain seated when we landed. Choking up and struggling with his words, he told us that our flight had the solemn duty of transporting the remains of a fallen U.S. serviceman home to his family. His uniformed escort was sitting a couple of rows in front of me and he was going to get off the plane first with the captain and join the family on the tarmac. As we landed the plane was quiet. No one stood except the soldier escort. The tarmac was full of fire fighters and other first responders with their equipment's flashing lights creating a surreal scene at the airport. Standing in lines. Saluting. There was a full honor guard from the military. People watched the ceremony out the plane windows and then once they got off the plane they watched from the gate area as the honor guard placed the flag-draped coffin in the hearse. The soldier's family was escorted over and at this point I turned away. I both wanted to show support but also thought this was a moment that didn't need witnesses.

It got me thinking. About how suddenly fragile our democracy feels. About how this young man had given his life defending it. About how no matter his personal politics he died for the ideal of American democracy. Which we really are in danger of watching fade before us.

I wanted to go back and give a more strident answer to the future of democracy: That it really hinges on the present. Harm is being done to democratic ideals in the U.S. and other nations. Is that harm reversible? Is it irreparable?

Whatever your politics are, you have to admit: Project 2025 has been an impressive, decades-long effort in foresight and activation. The Heritage Foundation and others determined a vision, crafted a plan, elected people at all levels of government, helped create a media ecosystem to support it, appointed judges, built grassroots, co-opted and cooperated with other movements and then, with power in sight, drew up a 900+ page plan. They are now faithfully executing that plan with purpose, intent and vigor.

The folks who go to SXSW are well-positioned to fight for our democracy, or to benefit from its reshaping. In many ways it's up to the people who were in Austin with me as much as anyone. Maybe it's incumbent on us futurists to not only imagine possible futures but to imagine better futures. Maybe it's incumbent on us futurists to help others around us visualize what a better future can look like. Maybe that would help? Clearly for some, this future we seem to be headed toward is personally better for them. But an incrementally better future for some who are already successful in the present, but one that comes at great cost to people who won't thrive under the new system doesn't seem truly better, does it?

So I'm going to be thinking, how can we use all of this energy and all of these smart people to make a difference.

Because I'm not quite ready to give up and say it's too late.

But I was also glad the audience wanted me to go dystopian on the future of democracy because that was a much easier future to imagine.

THE SCI-FI WRITERS
ON THE POWER OF IMAGINING THE FUTURE

Books are a gift. But author readings are an absolute treasure. Not only do the authors give you the book, but they often come to your town to read it with you, or sign it or talk about it, or all of the above. They're as concerts are to records, but usually way more intimate. They're a great way to meet your heroes and learn from them directly. Assuming your heroes are a bunch of authors, I guess. (I will now have Moxy Früvous stuck in my head.) I've told some stories in longer form, like Orson Scott Card and Douglas Adams, but I'll do these as a series of shorter vignettes.

T. CORAGHESSAN BOYLE

One of the best classes I ever took was a high school English class focused on Short Stories. The teacher put together an amazing reading list of classics of the genre and introduced two sections worth of avid readers to Carver and Cheever and Shirley Jackson and one author who became a particular favorite for me, T. Coraghessan Boyle.

I loved his short fiction and his novels and he, like Mitch Albom to an extent, showed that good writing can take you in a lot of different directions. Not just that he could be serious or funny, but that he could write short fiction and long form. He could also write non-fiction and tell really compelling stories that might not have sounded like the kind of set-up that would lead to a good story. If there's one theme that has often woven through his work it's the fragility and importance of our climate, and that of course resonated with my hippier high-school self and my futurism-leaning present.

I met him at, I think, a Borders book store (checks notes, in September 2000) with my friend Liz, who was also a fan. There were maybe 25 folks there?

NEAL STEPHENSON AND BRUCE SCHNEIER

A little earlier (May '99) I met Neal Stephenson. He was touring after the release of his book *Cryptonomicon*, which was a sprawling history of cryptography and World War II spanning 800+ pages. I devoured it in three days as I recall. He was going to do a signing at Stars our Destination, where I met Orson Scott Card. That was an incredible book store, dedicated to science fiction and fantasy and helped create community around these interests, too.

My roommate at the time, Jack, had a friend Sprite who worked there. She was a sweetheart, with green hair. Somehow she managed to sneak me in ahead of a lengthy line and get me a staff t-shirt commemorating the event that I still have.

Stephenson was touring with another author, Bruce Schneier, whose real-life cryptography scheme, Solitaire, was used in the book.

Later I would meet Schneier again at SXSW after a talk he gave there. His work at the intersection of tech and privacy couldn't be more important and it was fascinating to hear his talk and then chat with him a bit at the book signing later.

I saw Stephenson again right after things started to open up after the pandemic. He was touring then off of *Termination*

Shock, another climate-focused book. The premise of that story is kind of a scary one: What happens when today's "crazy" ideas don't seem as crazy anymore because tomorrow's reality has gotten so out of hand. It centers on an Elon Musk sort of character who takes climate action into his own hands because he's just gotten bigger and more powerful than most governments. The results of his actions have global consequences, creating winners and losers in the race to stave off climate catastrophe.

His talk was not what I expected. He gave a university-style lecture using PowerPoint to talk through some of the science behind the book! I asked a question during the Q&A about the Metaverse, a term he had coined a long time ago, but which was finally reaching a point of moving from science fiction to a technology exploding with possibility in the present.

Later, at SXSW, he did a fireside chat about the book and one of the points that came up in the discussion was that as dystopian as his book was, it was important to remember that we really have made a lot of progress on climate change. Projections made in the '80s and '90s spurred action that has actually slowed things. But also, that progress is fragile, too, as we're seeing today.

WILLIAM GIBSON

I haven't met William Gibson... yet. But I did get to interview him for *CoverStory*. His book, *Neuromancer*, coined the term 'cyberspace' and set an aesthetic for modem-based-hackerdom-cum-everyday-life-with-the-Internet in the 1990s and well beyond. He creates worlds that suck you in and make you dream of new things. And he did all of that while not being tech-savvy himself. Stephenson plunges into the worlds he writes about and creates, like the gaming research for Reamde or trying to understand cryptography and how it works. Gibson did less of that, but nonetheless imagined futures that have come to pass. You don't have to live and breathe a world to write about it. But as Stephenson shows, it can lead in different directions and different kinds of nuance when you do

Gibson also, decades later, was pretty accessible via Twitter and we had a fun back-and-forth with a couple Tweets about what to call alternative proteins of all things.

In pulling this together I dug out the interview I did with him of course, and I love the last question I asked him, especially in light of my current occupation: "Do you consider yourself a futurist?"

Here was his response, "I think of what I do artistically as exploration of new ways to apprehend the present ... I think I'm pushing back against what the late 20th century is doing to me. Better than trying to extrapolate or map where we're going. I never think of the things I write as being literally predictive. I think science fiction's predictive capacity is chronically overrated."

I'm really curious (and will try reaching out to see) if he still thinks this way. So many things he and many other writers, including the ones mentioned here, have written have seemed prophetic and, if nothing else, thought-provoking in a futurey way. I mean, what is Wikipedia if not the embodiment of the *Hitchhiker's Guide to the Galaxy*? Minecraft spun out from *Ender's Game*.... The list goes on.

And that's part of why I read Science Fiction. Not only is the best writing in the genre just plain good storytelling, but it puts me in a mindset to think about all the things that eventually led me to where I am now.

CARL BERNSTEIN
ON JOURNALISM AND COOLNESS

Bob Woodward and Carl Bernstein are the two *Washington Post* reporters credited with leading the investigation into the break-in at the Watergate Hotel, which eventually led to the resignation of President Nixon.

I have some mixed feelings about all of that.

On one hand, they inspired a lot of amazing journalism and journalists. On the other hand, a lot of journalists have since spent their careers trying to turn stories into the next ___gate. I'm not sure that's always the best goal. There's a difference in bringing light to problems in our institutions and letting the systems fix them vs. taking down the institutions.

A coworker recently made the analogy that the film about Watergate, *All the President's Men*, was to Baby Boomer journalists as *Almost Famous* was to Millennial journalists. That's an interesting analogy to me, especially, and I think there's something to the different kinds of inspiration these generations found.

I talked about *Almost Famous* from one perspective in the Dead Milkmen chapter. But its take on journalism and journalists is another good angle. Cameron Crowe wrote *Almost Famous*. It's based on his experiences as a young music journalist. I haven't met him – yet– but he'd be worthy of a chapter of his own.

I was already on my way as a GenX journalist when *Almost Famous* came out. Not surprisingly, it resonated. First, the killer soundtrack which used perfect songs, perfectly. The "Tiny Dancer" scene is Top 5 uses of music in a movie. Second, the idea that journalism can be a ticket to adventures. Coupled with that is the danger in trying to use journalism for access not only to events or concerts or experiences, but access to a lifestyle and a world of people you otherwise wouldn't know.

Maybe that works in politics? The White House Correspondents Dinner is a mixer for the press and the people they cover. Seems to be some legit mixing there. Or maybe that worked in the 70s? The Baby Boomers and their parents have done a bang-up job of pulling the ladders once they climbed them, after all.

Woodward and Bernstein did make themselves household names. That doesn't happen too often, but I think a lot of Boomer and other journalists hoped it would happen to them if they could just bring down a Name, or a Star, or even a Hero.

But *Almost Famous* was also the story of a different path I could have taken. Young William, the protagonist, is a would-be writer for a young *Rolling Stone* magazine. He thinks he has made friends with the band he's covering and their fan community. He thinks that he, like Woodward and Bernstein in a way, had become cool.

But *cool* is a real danger.

Then, in conversation with Lester Bangs (played perfectly by Philip Seymour Hoffman), he gets the best career advice a young journalist could get:

Lester Bangs: Aw, man. You made friends with them. See, friendship is the booze they feed you. They want you to get drunk on feeling like you belong.

William Miller: Well, it was fun.

Lester Bangs: Because they make you feel cool. And hey. I met you. You are not cool.

William Miller: I know. Even when I thought I was, I knew I wasn't.

Now, "cool" here is relative. Working as a journalist, especially a music journalist, is very likely "cooler" than a lot of other jobs. But it's not "cool" in the way the people you cover are "cool." In a lot of cases, the people you cover are way cooler than you are, which is the whole point of the job. You're telling their story, not the other way around. Robert Plant, David Bowie, Madonna, Bad Bunny... how many of their songs are about that awesome rock critic they met?

The real Lester Bangs wrote some amazing things about Lou Reed, for instance. The two would spar in interviews but seemed to grudgingly respect each other. Lester wrote, "Lou Reed is my own hero principally because he stands for all the most fucked up things that I could ever possibly conceive of. Which probably only shows the limits of my imagination."

But they were talking to each other in an interview. They were both essentially being paid to be there. And it was Lester's job to write things like that.

When Lou would blather on about the Village Voice rock critic, Robert Christgau, or rock critics in general during his mid-show rants (cf "Take No Prisoners"), it seemed like it should have been beneath him to do so. And it really kind of was.

Lester should have Lou as a hero, Lou shouldn't really think about Lester much at all.

Journalists. We're uncool.

Wait. That's not entirely true.

Journalists. We're uncool. Except to each other.

Which brings me back to the Watergate Hotel.

I was in D.C. at the Online News Association conference. A well-funded start-up sponsored a party for attendees. They decided to do one of the coolest journalism things possible. They hosted the party on the roof of the Watergate hotel and hired Carl Bernstein to speak. (The following year they had Dan Rather speak at their event at ONA in Austin. Then Judy Woodruff the next.)

But here I was mingling with other journalists sipping cocktails with appropriately clever names like "The Wire Tap."

And then Carl Bernstein spoke. And he *was* cool. His speech was so good that I approached him afterward and asked if he had a copy he could send me (he said he only had his own notes). Somehow I got to join the small meet-and-greet afterwards, and got a signed copy of the book he and Woodward wrote, called *All the President's Men*. My kid would later read it as prep for a Model UN session, and now knows everything about Watergate.

Again, Bernstein is one of the rare journalists who transcended the field and became cool in a broader context. Inspiring both good and less productive aspirations in generations of journalists to come.

But even he was only cool to a point.

I ran into a friend from high school at that same conference, having not seen her in the intervening 20 years. She told me a crazy story about working for AOL covering the 2000 Democratic National Convention. AOL had a luxury suite at the stadium for its staff and guests. And this one older guy kept coming in and grabbing snacks and pop. He seemed to just be freeloading, so my friend kicked him out.

At which point her colleagues told her that she had just met Carl Bernstein, too.

Cool has its limits, and even for the coolest, sometimes that limit is just a couple free Pepsis.

NATE SILVER
ON THE UTILITY OF STALKING FOR INTROVERTS

It was the first decade of the century and data was *en vogue*. Baseball was embracing a new(ish) breed of stats (finally) that measured things that mattered more than the traditional metrics. *Moneyball* was a hit book and became a hit movie. *Freakonomics, The Tipping Point* and *Nudge* were books about data and research and combining data from different sources to better understand the world and people's behavior in it. Civic data – using public data for public good – was also taking off. Chicago was at the center of many of these movements. And then came social media and suddenly everyone had a dashboard for everything.

These books* (and eventually Nate would write a book like this too) had something in common that I love. They made you look at the world differently. Specifically, they made you look at things you looked at every day but notice them.

Granted, sometimes that can ruin said thing, like Paco Underhill's *Why We Buy*. That book was amazing in that it deconstructed the experience of moving through a store or a quick-serve restaurant. In so doing, it pointed out the things retailers still (and this book came out decades ago now) do wrong. The part that ruins everything is he then explains how totally simple it would be to fix the problems. Now, every time I open a straw by the big fountain drink machine and there isn't a small garbage can nearby for the wrapper I would so completely obviously have in my hand at this moment, I'm filled with rage. Paco is still a genius and I was honored to get to meet him when I realized I was driving by his office in New York and called to see if he was there. He graciously welcomed me in and gave me a tour. This might even have been the same trip where I shared a limo with Dan Ariely and he gave me one of the weirdest book promotion items I've ever seen. I interviewed him a few times over the years and wound up giving him advice on what to do in Chicago with his family when he was in town once. Dan's books, too, made you look at the world differently.

I was writing about all of this data stuff for *Crain's Chicago Business* (and later *AdAge*) and finding excuses when I could to hang out at 1871, the new small business incubator in town where all of yesterday's nerds were suddenly today's cool kids.

Enter Nate Silver. He was a young baseball junkie and poker player who got interested in political polling and modeling election outcomes. His first big feat was correctly predicting the outcome of Barack Obama's first election in 49 out of 50 states. His 2012 election forecast was also on point and led to memes about him being a witch.

Crain's Chicago Business named him a 40 Under 40 in 2008, before his forecast came true. Which meant he was invited to the ensuing cocktail party and networking event. As a staffer at *Crain's*, so was I.

I've talked about how showing up is a super power. That's a recurring theme in this series. I've discussed stalking, which is a not-nice way of putting a thing I do sometimes. Perhaps it's more tactical interception. Or intentional meeting... I am open to suggestions. It's actually a lesson I learned in journalism school. If you wanted time with Abe Peck, the legendary magazine professor and *Rolling Stone* contributing editor, you camped outside his office until he could see you.

But there's something super useful about going to an event where you know basically no one (or, in this case I knew my coworkers but not a lot of other people) with the intent of meeting one person.

If you're an introvert like me, it's like a diversion. You're not walking into a room filled with people you don't know. You're walking into a room with one specific person you want to meet in it... somewhere.

It's like you're on a mission. Because you are.

So I set out to meet Nate Silver. My goal was to connect and meet him and then later have lunch with him and get to know him better.

I accomplished that.

Tangent: The next year I would get more clever and pre-stalk the folks I was most interested in and write the profiles of them myself. Thus I wound up writing the profiles of Andrew Huff, who edited a popular blog called *Gapers Block*, and Andrew Mason, the founder of Groupon. Mason, too, became someone I would have lunch with from time to time even as his company ballooned like crazy. My favorite Andrew Mason moment came during his company's first earnings call. Here he is, talking to investors for the first time as a CEO of a publicly traded company. And during the call I get a notification that "Andrew Mason is now following you on Pinterest." It's certainly plausible that those notifications were not in real-time. But I like to think that he was bored and surfing Pinterest while his CFO talked financials. Because that version is hilarious, and also on point.

Anyway, back to Nate. Lunch with Nate Silver was crazy. He seemed so young and had so much of the world ahead of him. Offers were pouring in for all kinds of business ventures. He was going to move to New York and figure out what was next. But I found myself giving him advice like, "dude, get an accountant and a lawyer who specializes in all the things you are going to need." (That last bit came from the as-yet-unwritten Meeting the Goo Goo Dolls.)

Later we could keep in touch and try and fail to hang out when I was in New York.

But I reconnected with him after the 2012 election when his book dropped.

We did a video interview at the hotel he was staying at, which turned out to be a bit of a production. I had in mind to ask him if he was a witch and see if I could get him to wear a witch hat. That would have broken the Internet at the time. However I sensed he didn't have a sense of humor about it, so I didn't do the witch hat thing.

But with Nate, or Andrew, or Paco, or so many of the other heroes I've talked about, the formula is pretty simple: Do your research. Show up (that's most of the battle). Make a connection. Have some reason to keep the connection going. Don't make single-serving friends when you can avoid it. Follow up. Send an email with a thank you and a reminder of some things you talked about, or something interesting they said, or suggestions for something they might like to read or a podcast episode based on what you discussed. Offer to connect them with someone else they might find interesting.

All of this is really just good manners, but it's also important.

And when you get a chance to see the world, see it differently, and notice it more.

*note, when awesome books make you look at the world differently, sometimes that's because they're not entirely accurate in their portrayal of things. It's good to be curious but also good to remain skeptical.

EDWARD TUFTE
ON LEARNING A
LESSON THE HARD WAY

There's a difference between "meeting your heroes" and working with them. I learned this the hard way. I also learned that how you tell someone's story isn't always how they want to hear it.

In my attic/office is a piece of artwork that says, "Avoid not writing." On the back you'll find the initials ET. That's the artist. His name is Edward Tufte. Tufte is really *the* pioneer in the visualization of data and information, which is something that's rather important to my various careers, and something that my dad was also a bit of a pioneer in -- especially in the use of computers to create graphics.

When I was working at *AdAge*, I wanted to interview Tufte, but his press contact said he was too busy. So I asked *AdAge* to send me to one of his one-day seminars. He held these classes around the country. More than 260,000 people have attended over the years. During the class I approached him and asked if I could interview him. He wrote out his @yale.edu email in silver Sharpie and I used that to reach out to him directly, circumvent his "people" and set up the interview.

We did the interview over email, which wasn't something I really liked doing but the piece went well. I recall that he did his responses on an iPad while taking the train. Regardless, he liked how the piece turned out and he started following me on Twitter.

A year or so later, he was teaching his class in Chicago. As someone who travels a fair amount for work, I know that it's often pretty boring in the evenings. I thought it would be a bit of a dream to have him come to a Journalist Happy Hour, the networking group that Scott Smith and I hosted and you read about in the Ted Allen chapter. Naturally I did what I always do: I asked nicely.

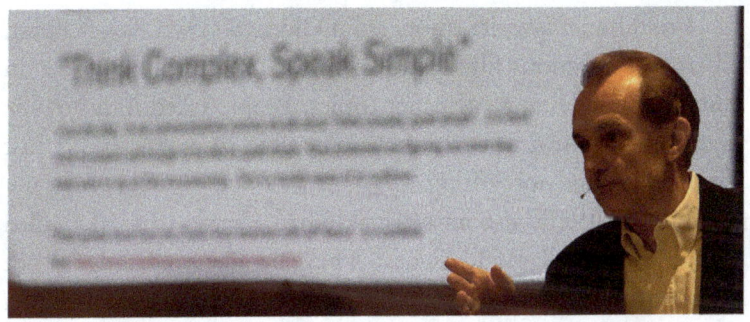

Tufte, presented. "Think complex, speak simple."

Amazingly enough, he said yes!

So it came to be that after several hundred people paid several hundred dollars apiece to hear his lecture, he came to a small bar nearby to chat with 25 or so of us. He told stories about working with NASA and also talked a little about journalism. He said something that sticks with me today and sums up a problem better than I've heard anyone else sum it up. Tufte pointed out artists and creators are getting paid less and less but platforms are getting paid more. The distance between creators (like musicians) and our money gets bigger and bigger as we pay Spotify but don't buy records. That system is broken and unsustainable.

But I digress.

Fast forward another year and he's coming back to Chicago again. This time I offer up a bigger ask: Dinner. One on one. And again, he accepts and invites me to join him at one of the restaurants at the hotel where he stays.

Over dinner we talked about writing, among other topics. He was working on his latest book and I had recently wrapped mine. One thing that struck me was his attention to detail. As a designer, he thought about how the line breaks looked on a page – while he was still writing. Usually that's the last thing you worry about, but he had it baked into his process.

I told him a favorite quote from Chicago's own Roger Ebert. Ebert was a famous film critic and was a very prolific writer on film and a wide range of other topics. People asked him how he was able to churn out so much incredible copy. He said, I just "spend less time not writing."

Now, Tufte is also an artist. He had a series of works called "philosophical diamond signs." They are like traffic signs, but with warnings about life rather than about traffic. I said as much as I loved the quote, it seemed a little long for a diamond sign.

Tufte got a twinkle in his eye. He loved the quote, and also loved the challenge. He pulled out a notebook and we began working through ideas. Eventually, we hit on "avoid not writing." It was true to both the intent of the original and also the double-negative structure of it.

Tufte had six copies made, and sent me one. It is one of my most cherished possessions.

The incredible thing, however, was that Tufte had been thinking about *me*. He'd enjoyed working with me on the *AdAge* piece and wanted to hire me to do some writing for him. Some would be ghost writing for his blog and site, and monitoring some of his social media.

This sounded like a dream, especially when he quoted me a generous monthly retainer.

He flew me out to San Francisco to attend his class there with the idea that I could write a public blog post on *Medium*, for instance, and he could link to it.

We had dinner again – this time at a California Pizza Kitchen – and he told great stories and gave great travel advice: Create a routine, use Bose headphones, buy the emergency row window AND the middle seat as a buffer. We talked more about process and writing. Again back to the recurring theme of habits and routines.

I attended his class and took part in his after-show ritual: He soaked his feet in ice water (I did not), and he had an egg cream and made me one, too.

Then I blew it. He really didn't like the piece and we basically never talked again.

Still, I got a great set of stories, learned a lot and have a unique piece of art to go with it.

I have a tremendous amount of respect for Tufte and think of his lessons regularly. He truly is one of the smartest people around and just operates at a different level from most. He has a smart head for business, the soul of an artist and the dedication to craft to produce on top of it. That's a rare combo at any level, let alone one so elite.

But yeah: be careful whom you work with. Working with someone isn't the same as friendship – which isn't to say that you can't be friends with coworkers. But it's a funny relationship, based on convenience and mutual benefit. It has a shelf-life based on how long you wind up working together. When that clock is up, or the mutual benefit becomes too one-sided, everything can disintegrate fast. I wish I had thought that through in this case. It's a rare bridge I burned, even if accidentally.

Back to the artwork: Writing is what I do. Doing it means avoiding not doing it. You might well do other things in your life and make a living that isn't based on words. But whatever you do, do it well, love doing it, and mostly avoid not doing it. It's the only way to get things done.

Tufte with his copy (1/6) of the piece we created together. He posted this on Twitter and retweeted my comment on his post.

(P.S. In Tufte's honor, I spent quite a bit of time editing this chapter to get the line breaks where I wanted them.)

THE POINTS GUY
ON BUILDING NOT JUST COMMUNITIES BUT EMPIRES

I suppose I could have been The Points Guy. It's the funny thing about getting into something before the Internet really existed. Sometimes I forget to go back now that there is an Internet and do the Internet things. But when you do, you often discover that there is a community around something you thought was just a thing you did on your own. That was true with Taylor Welden and Carryology and it's true with The Points Guy.

Like wait, there's advice? There's a subculture? There's a fandom? Who knew!

It's a weird generational thing I think.

But back in the 1990s I started earning frequent flier miles from credit cards. At that time, and man I feel old having to explain this, you could also get points from your long distance telephone service. They had sign-up bonuses just like the credit cards. Changing your long distance service wasn't that hard or inconvenient, like changing your cell provider is now. And I had two phone lines at my apartment. On one I actually made calls so I cared about long distance pricing on it and would try to find the cheapest provider. But I also had a line for my modem and never called long distance on that. So I'd flip the service every six months and get a new sign-up bonus. Which meant as a 20-something I flew to Europe First Class, for free. And I was hooked.

Again, it didn't occur to me that anyone else might care about this. But I was wrong.

Now, of course, fandom is everywhere on the internet. Connecting communities large and small. There are good things about that, and also darker things like disinformation. And for every harmless or helpful community, there seem to be dozens of groups of people you hope would never find each other in pursuit of mutual support and organization.

But I've both participated in and built communities (Prodigy message boards, Usenet groups, listservs and more) since the early days. I just didn't always go looking for them for everything.

Brian Kelly built a hobby of collecting travel loyalty points into a blog and then into a juggernaut. His site, The Points Guy, is a content machine and community wrapped into one neatly referral-linked package.

I knew I wanted to interview him for *WTF* so I did what I often do: I reached out, did some favors, made some friends by giving interesting people interesting challenges (in this case, some polls we did together). And eventually worked my way up to interviewing Brian himself.

And then I did the other thing I like doing, after an interview that was done via Zoom, I went out to meet him in person, too.

He was speaking at the Travel and Adventure show, a trade show in Rosemont, IL, where destinations come and try to convince you to spend your vacation dollars with them. You can learn about everywhere from the Bourbon Trail to Alaskan rail adventures to Costa Rican rainforests. And they have speakers. That's how we met Rick Steves, too.

Brian told the story of how he got his start and offered tips for travelers and other points collectors. During the Q&A I drifted over to the table where he was going to be signing autographs. Conveniently, I could still listen to the Q&A while also jumping the queue.

Brian seemed kind of new to doing public appearances like that. He didn't have a book, or anything obvious to sign. I had him sign my Admirals Club card, which seemed as appropriate as anything. I thanked him for the interview and told him it was nice to meet in person and suggested a couple of other things we could work on in the future.

The Points Guy and me. And yes, he's really that tall.

He hung out until he'd signed everything for everyone and we got a family pic, too.

MEETING MY HEROES
(MY DAD'S VERSION)

On July 3rd, 2025 I went to the Cubs game on my grandmother's (dad's mom) birthday. The Cubs were celebrating 100 years of Cubs radio broadcasts. I was joined by three friends from Northwestern, my (and my dad's) alma mater.

The game was against Cleveland, which is the team we beat to win the World Series in 2016. I watched some of those playoffs on the phone with my dad, and then called him from the victory parade which I watched next to the Jack Brickhouse statue outside Tribune Tower. At the game, current Cubs radio broadcasters Pat Hughes and Ron Coomer threw out the first pitch wearing jerseys numbered 100.

This was special for a number of reasons. To explain, I'll turn to an interview my kids and I did with my dad at Christmastime, 2018. In it, he talks about meeting some of his heroes. Here's how this went:

Andrew: Which sports team were you a fan of as a child?

MFC: I was a Chicago Cubs fan because my mom was when we lived in Chicago. [Editor's note: as mentioned earlier, my grandmother was a literal card-carrying die-hard Cubs fan.] We could take the L and go to Wrigley Field. We did that on what were called Ladies Days. This is when the people who went to baseball games were mainly men. So in order to have more women interested in the game so maybe they'd go with their husbands and take their kids, they created Ladies Day and ladies got in at a reduced price and if they brought their kids it was even better. So we'd get off the L and walk to Wrigley Field and go watch a Cub game during the day.

MLC: Were there some Cubs you especially remember seeing or some memorable games?

MFC: Ransom Jackson was one of my favorite Cubs, and Hank Sauer. They were all just great. I mean it was just such a wonderful experience to be watching with all that grass and fresh air.

| Andrew and I also got to meet Fergie Jenkins.

MLC: Did you ever see Fergie Jenkins?

MFC: Yeah I did. When I got older and went to work for WGN for a while, one of my duties was the backup producer for Cubs games. So I got to know Vince Lloyd and Lou Boudreau who were doing color and the play-by-play at the time. I went to a couple games when I could be in the broadcast booth. But that was before Harry Carey, "Take me out to the ballgame" so I didn't get to get involved in all that.

MLC: And Brickhouse too, right?

MFC: Oh yeah Brick was kind of...I wouldn't call him a friend but I certainly knew him. In the great snow storm of 1967 when you could barely move, I would pick up his secretary on the way to Bradley place and so she could go to work.

MLC: What were you doing with Jack Brickhouse in December?

MFC: I was also the backup producer for the Brickhouse show which was the afternoon talk show. And he would have celebrities and whatnot.

MLC: That segues really nicely into Jane's question.

Jane: What famous or important people have you known?

MFC: Probably the most famous one, besides Vice President Hubert Humphrey, was Maurice Chevalier. We did an interview with him in his hotel suite and I had a cold. So I was sort of chugging Robitussin. And by the end of the interview, which was little longer than an hour, I was pretty tipsy. I met him. I sat in and produced. When "Sing along with Mitch" was popular, he sat in for some one of our regular radio hosts and I ended up producing his show. I met Arlo Guthrie.

Vice President Humphrey was a special treat because we did an interview with him during the '64 election and he autographed a book for me and he had his dinner while we were doing the interview. His dinner was a cold cheese sandwich and an apple. This is the Vice President of the United States.

I worked for Lyndon Johnson and I met Ladybird. Lyndon Johnson was our President of the United States. I was the assistant director of the Radio Television News Service at the Democratic National Committee. We recorded all of his speeches no matter where he went through the Army Signal Corps and we would then produce an edited news digest of what he had to say. The White House did a transcript of all of his speeches and I was the official presidential translator because he came from West Texas and he sounded like my granddad. So the Eastern ladies who were actually doing the transcript didn't always understand what he had to say. I did.

MLC: Did you get to meet him?

MFC: No I never did. But we went to his Inauguration and we got on television when we did that. And my dad was asked by the President to work at the National Highway Transportation Safety Association. He had pictures of himself getting a bill signing pen. And we still have the pen [Note: of course we still have the pen].

RICK BAYLESS
ON FOOD AS A CONNECTOR

Restaurants are a place where you can sometimes meet your heroes. The first time I ever visited Vegas we did the things one does. We played blackjack. We explored the Strip. We watched the fountain. And we ate steak. Over an indulgent dinner, I said something obvious, that Vegas is the type of city where anything can happen at any time and I looked up and finished my sentence with... "Ladies and gentlemen, Mr. Ed McMahon..." As Johnny Carson's affable sidekick walked by as if on cue.

In *What the Future* we cover the future of a different topic each month. Most of those I have some interest in and some connection to. There have been exceptions, like the "Pets" issue, or the "Beauty" issue. But "Food" is especially tricky. I do eat food, but if you've ever had a meal with me you would not describe me as a foodie.

Granted, I've dined at some of the best restaurants in the world. I've eaten at Blue Hill Farm, one of the OG farm-to-table experiences. I brunched at Brasserie Les Halles, though sadly didn't meet Anthony Bourdain. I cosplayed someone who was a more adventurous eater and dined at Alinea. I did a tremendously poor job of neatly eating the dessert balloon but ate many of the other dishes.

I'd probably trade them all for one last double dog with fries on a Sunday night at Evanston's late Jim's Charbroil.

So yeah, doing the future of food is always a little tricky for me. But one of the most thoughtful interviews was always Rick Bayless.

Chef Bayless is a Chicago-based chef with a series of restaurants at different levels of complexity and price point. The flagship is Frontera Grill, an affordable Michelin Bib Gourmand. More upscale is the Michelin-starred Topolobampo. And he has a quick lunch spot called Xoco (which translates to "little sister") with tortas and other Mexican dishes.

My friend Natasha was originally a work friend but has stayed a friend friend since I left *Livability*. She was coming to Chicago for work so I suggested lunch at Xoco because I like showing off the best of Chicago when I can (though yes, I take folks to deep dish pizza, too). Meals are where we meet people. Or coffee (which I also don't drink).

As Bayless told me, "One of the things that is most important about gathering a group of people around the table is that it's like the microcosm of civilization, because there's no family where everyone fits together perfectly. You kind of learn, you know, to be civil to one another. You share really great moments together. The fact that nourishing ourselves is part of that codifies it in a very special way because everyone will tell you that one of the strongest senses is the sense of smell. I would say that the role of the table is creating memories and those memories are the ones that promote civilization."

So it was fitting to bring a friend to catch up at Xoco over an incredibly tasty meal. But I figured I should also explain why I chose this place, so I told her about who Chef Bayless is: He was one of the first "celebrity" chefs of the modern era. He and his wife Deann opened Frontera in the mid 1980s and shortly thereafter launched a cookbook of "Authentic Mexican" dishes. He's won lots of awards for cooking, but also for teaching and humanitarian causes. He's started non-profits. He worked to get federal support for restaurants as Covid hit and crushed the industry.

As I finished explaining this, I looked up and... "Ladies and gentlemen, Chef Rick Bayless." There he was. In retrospect, he was clearly coming from the airport. He had a hanging bag and backpack and I caught him off guard. But he was polite and I appreciated the chance to put my face to the voice on the phone and shake his hand and support his restaurant.

THE STORM CHASERS
ON WHY YOU SHOULD NEVER STOP CHASING... YOUR HEROES

The TV show *Storm Chasers* told the story of several groups of people who chased tornadoes, which, like sky diving, is a thing you can do if your life isn't exciting enough on its own. The show on Discovery seemed at first to be the story of a filmmaker, Sean Casey, determined to shoot an IMAX film from inside a tornado. He'd built a special tank-like thing with a camera turret to do so. It was called the TIV for "Tornado Intercept Vehicle." He was teamed with a group of meteorologists who were trying to create a 3D model of a tornado forming using Doppler radar (the DOW, "Doppler on Wheels"). They were led by a legit science guy, Josh Wurman. Another group was trying to deploy sensors in the path of tornadoes. This was the Twistex team. But the show eventually also starred a crazy, energy-drink-fueled crew who also had a tornado tank called the Dominator. Reed Timmer was also a young meteorologist but seemed at the time somewhat less serious than Wurman and certainly less well-funded. He was brash, and maybe rash but also quite good at finding tornadoes. His mantra is a good one: never stop chasing.

Pam and I watched the show in our early days of parenthood and couldn't get enough of it.

The scientists and filmmakers were doing incredible things and risking their lives to do so. It was clearly an adrenaline rush for Timmer and the Dominator, too. But they were collecting data to help better understand how tornadoes form and how to predict their genesis and paths.

Despite all their knowledge and experience, the Twistex team led by Tim Samaras was killed in the 2013 El Reno, OK tornado. It was the largest tornado ever recorded and its rapid growth proved too much for the team, who weren't in a particularly armored vehicle.

Casey eventually got his shot and made his IMAX movie, *Tornado Alley*. The film debuted at the Adler Planetarium in Chicago in 2011. He brought the TIV and Wurman brought the DOW. It was very cool to get to go and see the vehicles and meet the people behind the show.

I followed Reed Timmer on Facebook and hoped eventually that I would get to meet him, too. I never stopped chasing him, you could say. Finally in 2024 he came to town to give a talk at his niece's high school. Pam, sadly, was out of town on business, but I took two of the kids.

Timmer's talk was very low-budget. It was just him and a Powerpoint that didn't always work. He was on the floor. Literally our level. Not on the stage. There was nothing between him and the audience. Timmer said he wasn't afraid of tornadoes because they don't come after you like people or animals. You have to go find them, study them, observe and learn about them, and then you get to decide how close you're comfortable getting to them.

He talked about how it's tough to earn a living as a self-funded scientist and there's competition, but it's mostly a friendly community. And he showed lots of insane videos of driving into tornadoes.

I tried to model my Meeting My Heroes toolkit™ for my kids. We did our research. We showed up early to get a good seat. I took advantage of the fact that he was hanging out before the show and made an ask (photo and autograph). It wasn't a big ask, and Timmer clearly enjoyed making his fans happy. Afterward we were patient as we awaited our chance to sit in the Dominator itself. I mean, how cool is that? Sometimes you just stand around. Sometimes you get in line as fast as you can. Sometimes both happen.

Me in the Dominator

The kids watched and...didn't really participate. But at least they humored me. It's important to me that they see some of this in action. I hope to inspire them to meet their heroes, too. Or at least to have heroes. And to have plans. And to figure out how to make those plans actually come together. All of this has probably come through if you've read this far. But it's time to start saying the things out loud. Because each of my kids is pretty remarkable in their own way and what parent doesn't want great things for their kids?

For some, that's chasing storms. For others, chasing heroes, and lessons and most of all stories. Whatever you want to chase, you just have to practice, build muscles (or habits, or routines or rituals and skills) and have a plan to get there. Which brings me, oddly, to a professional trainer, who might be the least likely hero of them all if you've ever met me.

BUDDY MORRIS
ON THE BASICS

I never thought I would be the parent of an athlete, let alone a coach. Of a travel team, no less. Likewise I never thought one of my all-time favorite *WTF* interviews would be with a professional trainer. And then I met Buddy Morris – virtually anyway, although I still hope to meet up with him next time the Arizona Cardinals come play the Bears.

In the chapter about Ryder Carroll, creator of the Bullet Journal, I talked a lot about the importance of habits and routines. Buddy Morris and I chatted about that, too.

I admittedly haven't spent enough effort on my own health and fitness over the course of my life. I haven't eaten well. Sports were never my thing, even when I did try.

Now I've built some healthier habits. I still have work to do on that and advise my kids that it's easier to start those habits early than try to catch up later.

Buddy was a fascinating guy. It's easy to see a guy named Buddy and look at his headshot and form an opinion. But you'd be wrong in some key ways. This guy is a life-long learner. He studies his changing world of health and fitness every day, reading journal articles, trying new things. He talked about toughness but also about rest, and time restoring and recuperating. He talked about how he likes to walk in the grass of the field for "grounding" between meetings.

He's been a trainer since 1980, when he was conditioning future football Hall of Fame QB Dan Marino at Pitt.

I asked him if Then-Buddy was talking about rest, or grounding, or the importance of mental health. He said that Today-Buddy would fire that Buddy. And admitted that Then-Buddy then would probably fire Today-Buddy, too.

Buddy said one line in the interview that has stuck with me. I've quoted it to people in a lot of different contexts. He said, "The basics are the basics for a reason, because they work." He was talking about how "if you want to get faster, run sprints; if you want to get stronger, put more weight on the bar." (Side note: he would approve of a great but stupidly long *Men's Journal* article that says gyms and personal trainers are a scam and all you really need to do is lift weights.)

There are so many realms in which this idea of "the basics" applies. In a world where things change pretty quickly, remembering the basics comes in handy. It doesn't mean you shouldn't add new tools to the box, but it also doesn't mean to scrap all the old tools just because something new comes along. Do the work. Show up. Practice. Read widely. Build good habits and routines. Make the connections. Send that follow-up email, or text, or make that call. And again, surround yourself with interesting people.

If I've done this whole Meeting my Heroes thing right, these are all themes that should have come through, but if not I'm saying them all out loud here.

It's a good point to recap, because we're heading into the final lap of this adventure.

CHUCK KLOSTERMAN
ON FINDING INSPIRATION IN BOOKS

My dad's advice to...really to *anyone*, was to read. More importantly, he said, don't just read your favorite kinds of books. Read books far and wide that will challenge you and inspire your curiosity and creativity. He was right and I've applied that time and again. Here's a story of one of those books and the impact.

I read a book of short essays by Chuck Klosterman called *But What if We're Wrong*. The premise was, what if we think about the present as if it were the past. One hundred or 500 years from now, what ideas from our current era will still matter, or be covered in the history books. For instance, not even all of the most popular movies or music will still be talked about.

The idea really struck me, and I realized it was an interesting way to think not just about the past but about the future. All I had to do was flip it around. If you think about the future, what is something you're going to wish you had tracking data on. (Tracking data is when you ask the same question over time and see how the responses change.) It's a way to measure trends, which is a big part of what we do at Ipsos.

This little seed of an idea became the foundation for how we told stories about Ipsos and the work we do. Klosterman became the lead of a new Q&A series. I created my own grad school program by interviewing my new industry heroes, just like I had at *AdAge* and *Livability* before. The prompt about "what will you wish you had a trend line on" was the genesis of *What the Future*.

In short, the future-pivot of this one Klosterman idea in this one set of essays shaped the next several years of my career.

But if reading is about learning (and so is meeting your heroes), Klosterman told me something in that interview that was fascinating. He said people didn't question the book generally. But people who were experts in something would question the portion about the thing they were expert in.

He told me, "The more you understand something the more it becomes part of your identity and the less willing you are to see a less obvious reality. It's kind of a paradox. The more you know about something the less willing you are to learn about it."

ZOË KEATING
ON APPLYING STORIES IN UNEXPECTED WAYS

When I started *What the Future*, with that Chuck Klosterman essay in mind, I wanted to talk to people outside of Ipsos. This was for two reasons, one because it was the right way to tell the story. The other reason was selfish: I wanted an excuse to keep talking to interesting people and to meet more heroes.

I also wanted to bring in more perspectives than just those of people I worked with and their corporate clients. It worked amazingly well. My colleagues are super-smart people. But to pull in an audience, I wanted to borrow other people's networks. I also wanted to talk to the people that our readers were already reading.

I started by writing an issue about housing, talking to a lot of people I had met during my Livability.com grad school program. My first call was to Richard Florida because I knew if I got him, I could get anyone and I figured he'd say yes. I was right on both counts. From there it all fell into place. I interviewed CEOs, a former governor, a current mayor, professors, authors, artists, and Zoë Keating.

Zoë was the archetype for how I wanted *WTF* to work.

She's a cellist and I listen to her music all the time, especially while writing. But I didn't talk to her about music. Instead, we talked about the healthcare system. Her young husband had died from cancer. It was a tragic story, made more tragic by his awful experience with doctors and insurance and all sorts of complicated things. As that was happening, Zoë wrote about it on her blog and gained the attention of all sorts of important people including then-Vice President Joe Biden and his Cancer Moonshot.

She was the example I gave to my coworkers when I was pitching the *WTF* idea. People smiled and nodded. "Talk to a cellist about healthcare, uh huh. Sure."

Thus, when it came time to do the Healthcare issue I began my pursuit. It took months, but I didn't give up. She seemed interested so I just kept coming back to her.

She was touring so I went to one of her shows, knowing she usually signed autographs afterwards, so I could introduce myself and try to move things along (and also because I love her music and have written with it as a soundtrack for years). In the end, I got her scheduled and the story was sad, but perfect.

Zoë came to understand the medical system in a very different way than most people see it, owing partially to her background as a data and information architect. She told me, "Each patient is different. I'd want to know everything; that's my personality. But my husband would not. Sometimes there's a disparity between what a doctor needs to tell a family and what the patient needs to hear. I don't see that doctors think that they're responsible for that."

Zoë Keating is an amazing cellist. Seriously, what she does with computers and sound loops is so cool and mesmerizing and when I've seen her live I still couldn't figure out how it all worked.

But more to the point, when you want to learn about something you should absolutely 100% talk to the experts, or read what they've written. Dig into the data. Watch interviews on YouTube. Do your homework, in other words. Zoë did that to understand her husband's condition and the system that was trying to cure it.

I do that as prep for these (granted lower-stakes) encounters. But for my purposes, that all will only give you one critical part of the picture. To really understand an issue, learn not just from the people who shape it and guide the issue. Learn from the people affected by that issue. Get as many perspectives as you can. Because sometimes the strongest voices on an issue are on the outside, not the inside. And sometimes, the strongest voice is an instrumental.

AMANDA PALMER
ON THE BEAUTY OF ART

One of the most amazing text messages I ever got read:

> "hey ! it's amanda effing palmer. running a tad late: 2:10 ok?"

How did I get here?

My first outreach was through Twitter. Just trying to get on her radar. I Tweeted how much her album *There will be no Intermission* reminded me of Lou Reed's *Berlin*. Which is a high compliment. She Tweeted back, "Thank you Matt. 'The Kids' is the only song on earth that has never not brought me to tears. I listen rarely, it tears me apart."

I reached out to interview her for the "Beauty" issue of *What the Future*. We liked to have a "pivot" at the end of each issue to take you in a slightly different direction. For "Beauty," we moved from physical beauty, which was the subject of most of the issue and into more ephemeral "art as beauty." Amanda Palmer seemed a perfect person to have that discussion, especially as she had gone to a self-funded model for her work supported by fans through the Patreon platform.

We had our initial conversation backstage at her Chicago tour date and discussed what kind of survey question she would like to ask. She wanted to know if other people felt more beautiful when surrounded by beautiful things like art and architecture and nature (they do) or surrounded by beautiful people (they do not).

I shot the show, which was a treat, as was getting to do part of the interview in person.

But throughout my career I've tried to tie in the things I love and the thing I'm good at and apply all of that and all of this (waves hands at this entire project). I've written about music for Ipsos. I tried to interview Bowie as a "marketer of the year" for *AdAge* (he declined the honor) and did write about his online art gallery, Bowieart.com. Through the site I bought one of his Tarot Card series of lithographs, which they offered to upgrade to a signed version but stupid ethics made me decline. I had photos (including an impromptu shot of Oprah) appear in *Crain's* when I worked there. And perhaps most amusingly, I got will.i.am to write a column about "communiting" for *AdAge*. That led to a pitched battle with my copy desk which insisted on running a disclaimer after will.i.am insisted on us running the column as-is with his... unique sense of punctuation and capitalization.

It was great to meet Palmer. And to see her art in person again (I'd shot the Dresden Dolls back in the day). It was great to shoot the show and use those photos in *WTF*.

And it was a fantastic conversation, as I'd imagined it would be and which did indeed take place at 2:10.

She said, "I think human being mammals desperately need to feel un-alone and need to feel our experiences and losses, and our difficulty is reflected in one another. We forget how practically applicable art can be in our lives. We forget that the reason our ancestors came up with this bizarre idea in the first place was to help each other to make sense of the world, to make sense of pain, to make sense of the dark. Art is a fantastic vessel to carry that message of un-aloneness from one to the other."

I'd also interviewed her friend Zoë Keating in *WTF* and I mentioned that if Palmer thought the interview was fun and the free survey question was a good experience, maybe she could put in a good word for me with someone else she and Zoë knew, whom I dearly wanted to interview. I hoped she would realize that I wasn't trying to use her for her connections, but also that I would appreciate her connections. There's a nuance but a critical one there. I figured if anyone would get that, it would be the author of a book called, *The Art of Asking: How I Learned to Stop Worrying and Let People Help*.

In the end, I didn't get that other interview. As you'll see next, that turned out to be OK, maybe.

THE ONE WHOM I DIDN'T MEET
PERHAPS THANKFULLY

I was watching *Northern Exposure* with my family. There's an early scene where Maurice, the uber-masculine-yet-complicated astronaut town founder, is talking about how John Wayne was his boyhood hero. Right until he learned that Wayne didn't do his own stunts. When he learned that, he said, his hero was "given feet of clay."

Maurice is from a bygone era, portrayed on a show that itself is 35 years old. John Wayne was his hero. But so was the poet Walt Whitman. Here's what he said about Walt Whitman and heroes:

> "I don't give a damn if Walt Whitman kicked with his right or his left foot. Or that J. Edgar Hoover took it better than he gave it or that Ike was true-blue to Mamie. Or that God-knows-who had trouble with the ponies or with the bottle.
>
> We need our heroes. We need men we can look up to, believe in. Men who walk tall. We cannot chop 'em off at the knees, just to prove they're like the rest of us.
>
> Now, Walt Whitman was a pervert, but he was the best poet that America ever produced. And if he was standing here today and somebody called him a fruit or a queer behind his back, or to his face, or over these airwaves, that person would have to answer to me.

Sure, we're all human. But there's damn few of us that have the right stuff to be called heroes."

I have now written about 70,000 words about more than 75 of my heroes. Each story has been mostly complimentary. To go back to the original premise, if you are afraid to meet your heroes, or meeting them disappoints you, you should maybe get some better heroes.

The last two chapters were about heroes in their own right, Zoë Keating and Amanda Palmer. I was glad to tell their stories, and mine. But I was also hoping they could also help get me closer to my great white whale. (That's a reference to *Moby Dick*, which was written by Herman Melville. I have not read that book on the advice of my sister. However, Jane has always used "Extreme Ways" by the musical Moby as walk-up music in softball. Moby is named after Moby Dick because Moby was supposedly, but not really, related to Melville. I didn't meet Melville, of course, but I have met Moby.)

Anyway.

I agree with Maurice that people need heroes. I don't, however, think they have to be larger than life like John Wayne or astronauts. I think I've presented a pretty broad range of heroes in this collection.

America is obsessed with celebrity. Celebrities get conflated with heroes. We're bombarded by action films recycling old heroes like Super Man or making up new ones. Some of us grew up with flawed normies who became heroes like the "Greatest American Hero" or the Incredible Hulk.

We build our heroes up, sometimes. Part of the problem is maybe that we learn the hero arc in English class. We are surrounded by hero stories and try to make everyone out to be a hero, or an "everyday hero." We're taught that first responders are all heroes. And many, maybe even most of them are. But some... aren't.

Bowie was a hero every day and thought everyone had a chance. He sang that we can all be heroes, at least for one day.

But maybe we shouldn't try too hard. We should keep heroes rare and rarefied. Because heroes are people too.

Seventy thousand words in and I'm still wrestling with this idea of what a hero even is.

Part of the reason I'm wrestling with the definition is because of the one that got away.

Which brings us to Neil Gaiman.

Sigh.

I loved *American Gods*. I loved *Good Omens*. I loved his short stories. I loved him on Twitter (a fallen hero of a platform) and how human he was but also he was clearly just smarter and more clever and witty than the rest of us but still hung out on social media with us. He has replied to me on Twitter and retweeted things. Then he joined Tumblr!

He had a habit of signing his books in airport bookstores while waiting for his flights. Just casually popping in with his fountain pen and hoping no one would notice. He seemed to care a lot about his "stealth signings."

He Tweeted about doing this at LaGuardia one time. He actually got caught. His Tweet read, "I signed a bunch of copies of NORSE MYTHOLOGY today in NY LaGuardia terminal B. I DID talk to the shop assistant. Her: 'Er, why are you doing that?' Me: 'It makes people happy.' Her: 'Oh. Okay. I'll put them back on the shelf for you.' No police were called."

I was sitting in the New York Public Library soaking it in before a flight home. I read the Tweet, closed my laptop and hopped a cab to LGA. I searched a couple of book stores and nothing. So I Tweeted, "The guy at the pre-security store wishes you had specified which gates or airline. Heh. He's had three people ask so far."

@NeilHimself REPLIED in a timely fashion, "Air Canada

area," and I then had to talk my way through TSA with a boarding pass for the wrong part of the terminal. I think the TSA guys determined I was too much of a nerd to be a threat. And that's how I came to own a signed copy of *Norse Mythology*, which I still treasure.

I have so much respect for him as a writer. I loved his turn on Master Class. Kids (though not mine) grew up with *Coraline*. My kids didn't love that book. But they did love watching *Good Omens*. My kids grew up hearing me talk about him; we watched in the pandemic as he did a virtual book signing of *Pirate Stew* with the illustrator, Chris Riddell. I drove to Madison to finally see him in person at a reading he did, and I bought each of my kids their own signed copy of his "Make Good Art" graduation speech.

I came close to interviewing him for *What the Future* but eventually was rebuffed. Twice.

I kept trying. Hoping I'd have the right hook or angle to get him to bite.

And then....

The first allegations surfaced. And then the *New York Magazine* piece ran. In an actual way, Neil Gaiman is someone Maurice would have considered a "pervert" at best. At worst, he was a lot worse. [Note, he denies the worst bits.]

So I'm ending this series of *Meeting my Heroes*, with the one I wrestle with. I mean, what if it turned out that Lou Reed or Robin Williams were not great humans? From all accounts they were (Lou was maybe challenging for some...). But what if...

Everyone needs to do their own calculus about canceling artists and what happens to their work. Netflix and Amazon did their math and cut ties. Neil even stepped away from the work (TV's *Good Omens*, and the graphic novel that was being created) in the hopes that the art could continue without him. I had supported the *Good Omens* kickstarter to get a copy for one of my kids and we were given the option to withdraw when the allegations surfaced. I asked if we should keep the pledge. The verdict:

as long as he wasn't personally profiting in any way, it was still "good art."

He wasn't, unlike, say, JKR, so we kept our pledge.

"Make good art" is still a good mantra. *American Gods* is still a good book with a powerful idea about technology. *Good Omens* and *Sandman* are parts of the fabric of our world.

In the end, it's math, and choices and trade-offs. And the heroes we want to meet. Neil's sadly not a hero anymore. At least as a human.

Yet I'd like to ever give as good a speech as Make Good Art.

Had I met him, had I landed that interview, or a sit-down in Madison with him (I did see my friend the Mayor, with whom I always had good conversations), I would have been tempted to include it here. The conversation would have been brilliant and full of life lessons. Because that's how he is and what we would have talked about.

Also in the end, and this is the end for now, everyone would write this differently. Everyone has a different constellation of stars. A different pantheon of heroes. I hope you've learned something about mine, and something about me in the process.

Your views of what makes a hero and what doesn't will vary.

However, dear reader, to go back to the spoiler from the introduction, I hope you surround yourself with interesting people and meet as many of your heroes as you can. If you've chosen well, they won't disappoint. If you can't meet them, read about them. Listen to them on podcasts. Soak up what you can where you can. It's all worth it, I say watching a six-hour documentary on Billy Joel, whom I haven't and likely will never meet.

I have told a lot of stories. All of which are my story.

There's an idea that gets attributed in various ways to various people but boils down to, "the author is necessarily the hero of his own tale." In today's parlance it's having main character energy or vibes.

So yeah, I'm the hero of my story. That means in some ways you've met me too. I get that it's an odd way to tell my story.

There are huge parts missing. I haven't told the story of my friends really. Or my family. Therefore you haven't heard about the people who are really important to me day-to-day and decade-to-decade. They are the interesting people I surround myself with all the time.

Maybe those stories come next?

You've seen some people who you might kind of know already, but now through my eyes. And a bit of me through my eyes. Which is fitting for a journalist, eh?

Mostly you've succeeded in taking my dad's advice. If you've made it this far, you're a reader.

And that's the best note I can think to end on.

EPILOGUE: CAREER DAY

ON SUMMING IT ALL UP

In the back of my head, the "Meeting my Heroes" newsletter could be a lot of things: A book. A podcast. A TED talk. And hey look, the book happened! As for speaking, I did get a chance to try this in front of a demanding audience. The venue was perhaps unexpected. Or perhaps perfect.

I introduced Meeting my Heroes to...middle school career day.

It is, after all, the story of my career in many ways. So I told the kids versions of several of the stories here as I talked about what journalism is, its importance, how I practice it, and lessons I've learned along the way. All through the lens of these heroes.

I asked the kids who their heroes were for starters and got a lot of one-name stars: LeBron. Taylor. Mom. Jesus.

Some of the kids didn't admit to having heroes, but I hope they were just being shy. It's good to have heroes.

I started by telling the David Bowie story because I ~~figured~~ (hoped, and was proven correct) that of my heroes, he was the one the most kids would know.

Then I talked about how I didn't really ever have career goals in a traditional sense of "here's what I want to be when I grow up." Partially, I said, that was because my first job out of college was in a career that didn't exist when I entered college. My first job involved publishing on the Web!

I did want to get my name in *Rolling Stone* by the time I turned 30. I got there, but even that wasn't as I expected. It was a photo credit, not a byline. I also retroactively added, "publish a book before 40."

So no set goals, but rather I had values and things I thought would be attributes of a good job/career. I suggested they would develop their own list over time, but for me I wanted to work places where:

- I would have good stories to tell
- The job would keep me curious
- I wouldn't do the same thing every day
- I wanted something that would attach me to communities, or where I could build them myself
- I wanted to build things, not just maintain them
- And I wanted to always have new things to learn, new challenge, or sometimes just new walls to bang my head against

I told them journalism was my ticket to that and that I'd achieved all of those goals and then some. Speaking and travel could have been on that list as well, for instance. I checked those boxes, too.

I told some of the stories from Meeting my Heroes and brought it back with lessons from those stories. Finally, I had them be journalists and ask me questions. I gave some examples of good starter questions and the foundations of the Ws. They asked some good questions.

I said in the preface that this wasn't just about meeting people, it was about learning from them. Hopefully that carried through. With that in mind, here are the words of advice I left the kids with, based on some heroes I introduced them to.

1. Figure out your goals and priorities (Doc)

2. Go big or go home (Dr. Welch)

3. Be ready for the chances that come, and make your own (Steve Yahn)

4. Find your motivators (For the talk I broke Prof. Mary Ann Weston out, but she's included in Steve Yahn's chapter)

5. Make the relationships that count. Don't burn bridges, build them (Poi Dog Pondering)

6. Find ways to have fun (This was a big rocknroll.net digression but really comes down to the lessons in the Wilco/Lounge Ax chapter)

7. Use what you have to give back (The Calendar)

8. Show up, do the work, make the big ask (Richard Florida and Amanda Palmer)

9. Build your network, find the connectors and be a connector (Amy Webb, Ted Allen, Taylor Welden)

10. Your heroes are not necessarily your friends. This was mainly about Edward Tufte, but the Carl Bernstein and Dead Milkmen chapters touch on some of this, too.

11. Surround yourself with interesting people. This was the whole book, but especially The Mayors Emanuel.

Sure, it was middle school and the end of the year at that so I won't pretend they were all raptly attentive. Overall they were great kids and great listeners and different pieces seemed to hook different kids differently.

I should add that the setting was a little bittersweet.

I often think about the idea that we celebrate a lot of firsts but never know when something was the last until it's often long over. This time, I think I saw it coming. As my youngest are leaving that school, it's probably the last time I set foot in the place where my kids have spent so much time, had so many great teachers, maybe met some heroes for themselves and continued building their own stories toward who they will grow up to be.

And further, it's hard to get invited into the high school. My kids sat in on one of the five sessions I got to give, and that's also likely the last time I'll see any of my kids in a classroom.

Today's world really distances the parents from the classroom for a lot of mostly not-great reasons. So I'm glad I seized the chance, and I hope that maybe I helped nudge a kid or two in a direction or two. If not, well, I enjoyed the experience myself.

Who knows, maybe someday one of those kids will tell their kids about the day they decided they wanted to get into journalism.

I mean, I can dream still, right?

ACKNOWLEDGMENTS

"Meeting my Heroes" tells a lot of stories. In the end, it's my story in many ways. My career had an odd arc, with some places where it looped back on each other. There were through lines, however. Really, it's all about an interest in people.

And if you've read this far, you've also noticed that there were nudges, prods and doors held open. Every opportunity built on the one before it. So the acknowledgments will be a little long.

Of course it started with my parents and their support, including putting me in a position to succeed and sending me to Cranbrook. My mom is a story teller and keeper of histories. My dad certainly was too. At least... other people's stories. Part of the genesis for this project is rooted there.

I mentioned that part of it was also rooted in an idea from my friend Scott Smith, so I'm thankful he graciously let me borrow it.

Teachers were inspirations in many different ways.

I wrote about a couple of them directly but should also thank many of my Medill professors. Buck Ryan, who was set to oversee an independent study about the future of journalism in the dawn of the Web. When he left Medill, he introduced me to Abe Peck, the legendary magazine professor who agreed to help take over the project. Buck also introduced me to Alison Scholly who turned my independent study into a paid internship and later also became one of my professors and mentors.

More practically and later in life I learned much from Richard Florida, Kevin Stolarick and Steven Pedigo (who taught the economic development program I attended at NYU) and Andy Hines, who leads the foresight program at University of Houston.

A lot of opportunities stemmed from the editors I worked with: Starting at *AdAge* with Steve Yahn, Scott Donaton, Debbie Williamson and Abbey Klaassen and Allison Arden when I returned;. Jen Bulat at *CoverStory*; The folks at *Addicted to Noise* edited by Michael Goldberg; Isaac Josephson at Rolling Stone.com; Joe Cahill and Brandon Copple at *Crain's Chicago Business*; Bob Schwartzman, Natasha Lorens and Casey Hester at *Livability*; and Jonathan Cohen at Billboard.com.

Many thanks to all of the folks in the music biz but especially those who let me shoot for them: Joe Shanahan and Jennifer Lizak at Metro; Tom Lisack at WXRT; and of course Pam Morin, then marketing director for the big concert promoter, who introduced me to folks, hyped me, supported me and helped get me hired at Tweeter Center as its first House Photographer.

My favorite sandbox for photography has always been shooting Poi Dog Pondering. That's because Frank, Chaka and the rest of the Poi family "let me practice my art with the same freedom that they practice there."

Ipsos has given me extraordinary opportunities and super powers. That all started with the trust of Jim Meyer and Liz Knight and blessing of Pierre LeManh. That continued through Anne Farrer, Julia Clark, Amy Fenton, and of course Jessica Gates and an array of amazing leaders and partners, especially Chris Jackson and Mallory Newall. My team of Kate MacArthur, Ben Meyerson, Christopher Good and Zoe Galland have made *What the Future* what it is as well as all of my broader MarComs colleagues.

I've also had mentors and friends who contributed to all of my hero meeting and lessons learned including: Amy Webb, Peter Frances and Dante Chinni.

Pam gets an additional thank you, of course, for supporting so many of the crazy missions that led to the stories here.

And my kids, who are all heroes in their own right, and who inspire me to keep having adventures and keep telling stories.

This began as a newsletter, which led me to write this in the open, in installments. Thank you to the readers and subscribers and everyone who bounced an idea or caught a typo. Production of the book itself was funded by a Kickstarter. I clearly couldn't have done this without the support of the backers.

My sister, Elizabeth, graciously offered to proofread the book. I should note that I made some changes after she was done and I didn't let her have back at it so if you see anything amiss, that's ~~prolly~~ totally on me.

Clara Davis designed the awesome cover. She's a student at the School of the Museum of Fine Arts at Tufts University. You can hire her to design things for you, too!

Stephen J. Serio once again took my author photo and I can't recommend his photography enough.

And a final massive thank you to Robert K. Elder, my friend, neighbor and now publisher and quite a prolific author himself. He gave this book a home, and gave me a lot of good advice on getting it in your hands.

Deciding what meetings to include or not include wasn't easy. Maybe I'lll share some others in the newsletter eventually like: riding in a limo with behavioral economist Dan Ariely; or meeting urbanist Joel Kotkin, who told me that you should never underestimate the power of inertia; or getting a tour of retail guru and keen observer of humans, Paco Underhill's, Manhattan office on a serendipitous drive-by pop-in; or shooting the birthday party for Bon Jovi guitarist Richie Sambora at the Four Seasons; or hanging out backstage with Sting; or the Polyphonic Spree and meeting Tim again at SXSW; or a strange vibe during a post-show interview with the Red Hot Chili Peppers after Shirley Manson from Garbage flipped me off... Or.... Or....

But for now, I'll stop and say a sincere thank you to you for reading. You all are my heroes for getting to the end of these tales.

ABOUT MATT CARMICHAEL

Matt Carmichael is a writer, photographer, speaker and lifelong journalist. He has had a prolific freelance career as a writer for Addicted to Noise, RollingStone.com and Billboard.com, etc. and "day-jobs" editing at *AdAge*, *Crain's Chicago Business*, *Livability* and *What the Future*. His first book, *Buyographics*, was an Amazon Best Seller.

Matt has been called "an actual photographer" by Dave Barry and an "internet guru" in *Rolling Stone*. A former U.S. Census Bureau director said Matt's work was important for the nation. An Emmy-winning cellist said, "Matt Carmichael is one of those people you wished lived nearby so you could invite him to every dinner party."

As a photojournalist his work has appeared in *Rolling Stone*, *Spin*, and hundreds of other publications around the world. He was House Photographer for Metro, Tweeter Center, Charter One Pavilion and WXRT. He is the band photographer for Poi Dog Pondering. His photos have appeared in galleries, hung in private collections as well as decorating backstages at Chicago's largest concert venues. His work is represented by Getty Images and can be seen at rocknroll.net, one of the oldest and longest-running sites on the Internet. It launched in March, 1994.

Currently, Matt is an SVP at Ipsos where he leads or co-leads the largest and most impactful public trends and foresight projects.

He is a graduate of Northwestern University's Medill school and was awarded a certificate of achievement from the University of Houston's Foresight program.